CASTING YOUR NET

CASTING YOUR NET

A Student's Guide to Research on the Internet

H. Eric Branscomb
Salem State College

Allyn and Bacon
Boston • London • Toronto • Sydney • Tokyo • Singapore

Vice President: Joseph Opiela
Marketing Manager: Lisa Kimball
Production Administrator: Susan Brown
Editorial-Production Service: Omegatype Typography, Inc.
Composition and Prepress Buyer: Linda Cox
Manufacturing Buyer: Suzanne Lareau
Cover Administrator: Suzanne Harbison

Copyright © 1998 by Allyn & Bacon
A Viacom Company
160 Gould Street
Needham Heights, MA 02194

Internet: www.abacon.com
America Online: Keyword: College Online

Library of Congress Cataloging-in-Publication Data

Branscomb, H. Eric.
    Casting your net : a student's guide to research on the Internet /
  H. Eric Branscomb.
      p.   cm.
    ISBN 0-205-26692-4 (pbk.)
     1. Report writing—Data processing.   2. Research—Data processing.
  3. Internet (Computer network)   I. Title.
  LB1047.3.B74   1998
  371.3′028′1—dc21   96-38054
                                          CIP

Printed in the United States of America

10   9   8   7   6   5   4   3   2   02   01   00   99   98   97

Credits begin on page 176, which constitutes a continuation of the copyright page.

CONTENTS

DEDICATION

Even in these collaborative times, when instant communication is the norm and it seems you can't escape your email even if you try, writing a book can be a lonely undertaking. But there are many, many people who have helped make it less lonely for me, who've given me inspiration and ideas, who've selflessly shared their knowledge and expertise and encouragement.

I'd first like to thank the editors at Allyn and Bacon: Joe Opiela for continuing to believe in me for all these years; Kate Tolini for always being cheerful regardless of the problem I dumped in her lap; Allen Workman, the book doctor, for discovering me and getting me started and keeping me on a short rein. Allyn and Bacon's reviewers were helpful as the book developed: John M. Clarke, Bowling Green State University; Christine Hult, Utah State University; Mike Jackman, University of Louisville; Ed Klonoski, University of Hartford; and Gail Matthews-DeNatale, George Mason University.

I'd like to thank some special colleagues at the schools where I've taught over the past twenty-something years: Tom Newkirk, Donald Graves, and another fellow at the University of New Hampshire and its most wonderful writing program; Virginia Polanski at Stonehill College; Donnalee Rubin at Salem State College. To all my friends in the New England Alliance for Computers and Writing—especially Deb Burns of Merrimack College and Phil Burns of Worcester State College—thanks for your enthusiasm and scholarship. To my online friends and colleagues, far too numerous to mention, on ACW-L and MBU and all the MOOs—you've constructed me and this book in ways you'll never know. And thanks to Rick Rhodes of the Manchester, NH Apple Computer Users Group for introducing me to all those research sites I'd never have explored otherwise.

My family of course—no book could be written without an astonishing amount of support from one's family. My wife Sue; thanks for having the wisdom and patience for supporting me when I needed supporting, for encouraging me when I needed encouraging, for humoring me when I needed humoring, and for avoiding me when I needed avoiding. :-) To my eldest, Adam and Alison, college classes of 2000, thanks for believing. To my youngest, Scott and Lauren, too young to really understand where I was all those late nights and early mornings, a huge, printed thank-you that will be here when you're older. And my mother and father—you started it all, and kept it going, and never once doubted the value of teaching and learning. Thank you, all.

When, many years ago, I first arrived at the University of New Hampshire, it wasn't long before I came to know an imposing Hemingwayesque man who perhaps more than anyone else nudged my life in the direction it has since taken. He taught me the art and craft of teaching (though I'll never learn them as well as he taught them), the dignity of students and the dignity of their words, and the pain and joy of writing and teaching writing. Long before the Information Age had a name, he taught me to honor information; he insisted I tell the truth; he first encouraged me to write publicly. He gave me the single best piece of advice on my writing I ever received: "Surprise me." And so this book is dedicated—surprise!—to Donald M. Murray, the best teacher.

PREFACE

This is not another book on "The Internet": if you've checked the shelves of your local bookstore lately, you know that there are plenty of those books out there already. This is a book on how to conduct academic research on the Internet: how to find information, how to evaluate it, how to use it in your writing.

You've heard of the information superhighway, probably more than you care to. You're probably vaguely aware that there is a lot out there on the Internet, but you don't know where to find it. Maybe you have tried to find something and have been so overwhelmed and frustrated that you've given up. "There's too much out there," you may have decided, "All I want is a little information and when I try to find it I get 20,000 places to look, and most of it is commercials with pretty pictures or useless chitchat." Or perhaps you've looked and haven't found anything at all. The Internet can seem like the world's largest library, and it has no card catalog! You're standing at the front door, with a research paper to write, and you don't know which way to turn.

The Internet is truly a wonderful medium. Think of it: millions of computers all around the world, linked together. If you have a computer you can get the information stored on another one, you can write to people all over the world, and you can engage in multiple conversations on just about any topic imaginable with others all around the world. And you can conduct research at 3:00 a.m., in your pajamas, with cold pizza at your side, if you want.

On the other hand, the Internet is huge, it's confusing (especially to those not in on its secrets), people who seem to know how to use it talk funny (babbling nonsense like *URL* and *gopher* and *http*), and it's getting too commercialized. Most of all, even though you're convinced that the information you want is probably out there, somewhere on one of those millions of computers, you can't find it. In a perfect world, you'd be able to say to your computer, "Find me all the information there is on endangered species," for example, "and don't give me anything else." And your computer would say to you, "Yes, Master," and do it. However, the world and the Internet are not (as yet) perfect, and finding information on the Net is a skill to be mastered.

Much of the hype you hear about the Net today seems to imply that it's radically new, that there's never been anything like it, and that it will change your life in unimaginable ways. There's probably some truth in this, but it's more useful at the outset to think of the Internet in more familiar terms—not how it's different, but in what ways it's similar to things you're familiar with. You're familiar with the Yellow Pages, with libraries and card catalogs; you're familiar with books and their indexes and tables of contents. So wherever possible, this book will stress how the Internet is similar to things you already know.

In *Casting Your Net* I have tried to emphasize the skills of query construction and keyword searches. Most of the search engines available use some variation on the keyword search, often supplementing the searches with boolean logic. I have tried to give a solid introduction to these skills, for, given current technology, they are the skills most necessary for searching the Internet.

A couple of caveats about the approach and the intent of *Casting Your Net:* it takes for granted you know (or are in the process of learning) the fundamentals of academic research. This book alone will not teach you how to write a research paper. It assumes you have some general knowledge of computers and the Internet—you have an Internet account and you have used it some. If you want to know how to set up your computer, use a mouse, or make a webpage, there are books for that.

This book also assumes that you have access to the Internet, that you know how to use your computer, and you know how to use its software. You won't find any instructions on configuring your computer, on sorting out the mysteries of newsreaders or Web browsers, or writing HTML code. Again, there are plenty of good books already.

Casting Your Net will show you how to find information on the Internet, how to analyze and evaluate it for usefulness and validity, and how to use it in your writing to clarify, both for yourself and your audience, your ideas.

"As of this Writing . . . "

One of the real advantages of the Internet is its ability (in fact, its insatiable drive) to change rapidly, to keep up with things. And one of the problems in writing a book about the Internet is the impossibility of keeping up with the it. As I was writing this, some of the topics about which I'm writing went through two or three radical changes. The version of WebCrawler I started writing about is much different from the version I finally ended up illustrating; it literally changed overnight. It was a different service one morning than it was when I went to bed the previous evening.

Most of the pictures of various screens you will encounter in this book will have changed by the time you read this. There were times when it seemed as if every sentence I wrote needed to be preceded with "As of this writing . . . " because I knew that things would be different by the time this book got to you. Some of the details will have changed—what a particular service offers or how a particular search operates—but the general principles of searching the net won't change, nor will the necessity to develop a critical, questioning approach to what you find there.

CASTING YOUR NET

1

ACADEMIC RESEARCH AND THE INTERNET

If you're doing serious research, probably for a course assignment, and are dissatisfied with the amount and quality of information the library is able to supply, are curious about what's available on this new information medium you're hearing so much about, or just want to do most or all of your research from the comfort of your own desk and your own computer, then Internet research is for you. Using electronic on-line sources such as commercial services (for example, America Online and CompuServe) or the worldwide network of computers known as the Internet can greatly expand the range of information you are able to access. You may already be paying for a commercial account; if not, you may be eligible for a free Internet account through your college or university. Either way, you have access to an unimaginable wealth of information, ranging from the latest, most exciting, and most authoritative to the irrelevant, trivial, and incorrect.

Researching a topic for a term paper or other project using the Internet is actually similar to using print or other sources. As with any information, you can evaluate and synthesize the information you derived from Internet sources, use it in appropriate places in your paper, and cite it. But Internet sources present their own unique surprises and difficulties: though the information may be far more up to date than is possible in books or even periodicals (books can take years from inception to bookstore), much of the information you find on the Internet has not been reviewed, which means that no independent, knowledgeable person has examined the material you're reading and checked it for flaws or errors. That means you must do this, and you may not have that expertise.

A story continuously makes the rounds of the Internet: a young boy in England named Craig Shergold is dying of a brain tumor; before he dies, he wants to be listed in the *Guinness Book of World Records* for most get-well cards received, and asks that everyone reading this notice send him a card. The story is moving and sincere, and anyone reading it is spurred into sending a card. However, the truth of the matter is that Craig set the Guinness record long ago, has miraculously and fortunately recovered, and needs no more get well cards. The small local post office is swamped with hundreds of thousands of cards from well-meaning people around the world, despite pleas to stop from nearly every known authoritative source. The cards continue to arrive by the trainload while the original story is repeated over the Internet by people who want to help, perpetuating the problem. How could you know that the story is no longer true? What about the supposed cures for AIDS, the statistics on the supposed racial superiority of one or another race, the million and one other stories and statistics you can find—are they true or not? Is the statistic thrown about on a particular newsgroup a sound fact, derived through careful research, or is it simply a fabrication of some deranged person's mind? It is often difficult to know with any degree of confidence.

The Internet, since no one owns or technically even manages it, is an unruly thicket of information stored in a wide assortment of formats on computers all around the world. To someone attempting to use it, therefore, it presents a variety of faces: the simple transfer of information using ftp, the menus of choices in Gopher, the colors and maze-like connectiveness of the World Wide Web. The bad news is that, unfortunately, there is no card catalog, no easy way of finding the information you want. But the good news is that each of the major modes of accessing the Internet has its own way of searching for and retrieving information, so you're not condemned to random browsing in the hope you'll find what you need. These small, publicly accessible computer programs that allow you to look for information are collectively known as *search engines*. Each of the major online services has its own ways of searching its databases and information services, as well. For Internet searches, some of the search engines you'll likely be using are Archie, Veronica, WAIS, Excite, and Yahoo.

THE TWO MAJOR INTERFACES

There are two general interfaces for accessing the Internet. Depending on the type of computer system you use, they require significantly different approaches. Probably the most common (though it's becoming less so) is the command-line interface. You control the actions of the computer by typing commands on a line. If you've used MS-DOS machines and typed commands at a prompt such as "C:\>" you've used a command-line interface. Later refinements allow you to make selections from a menu by moving a highlighter up and down using the arrow keys on your keyboard. Conducting Internet research using this kind of interface is difficult and unwieldy because you have to memorize a number of commands. With this kind of account, your computer or terminal—wherever it is located—is nothing more than a "dumb terminal," a keyboard hooked to the college's mainframe computer where your account resides. This is a crucial concept; essentially it means that you are controlling a computer (other than the one at which you're sitting) and whenever you *download* or retrieve, a file from another computer elsewhere in the world, you are merely copying it to your account on the mainframe, not to the computer where you're sitting. And unfortunately, using that information you've just downloaded from Australia, for example, requires additional steps, which will be covered later.

More recently, owing to the development of the Macintosh and Windows graphical interfaces, using a computer in general, and conducting research in particular, have become easier. Computer screens are dynamic and colorful, and the computer is controlled by clicks of a mouse rather than memorized, typed-in commands. Furthermore, rather than being a dumb terminal, with this type of account (technically called a SLIP or PPP account) your computer is actually directly connected to the Internet, so downloads come directly to your computer.

The entire Internet may be accessed using either interface—command-line or graphical—but a graphical approach is generally more convenient and therefore is becoming standard.

THE INTERNET DOMAIN NAME SYSTEM

With tens of thousands of computers networked all around the world, there needs to be some systematic way of naming and differentiating each one so it is possible to easily and quickly find a particular one. This is made possible on the Internet by a system called the *Domain Name System* (DNS). Essentially, it allows for each computer on the Internet to have its own address, much like the post office's system of states, cities, streets and house numbers allows each building to have its own unique address. Internet addresses are composed of units separated by the symbol "." (pronounced *dot*) and read hierarchically from left to right, from most specific to most general. For example, the domain name for NASA Information Services is www.gsfc.nasa.gov. This means it's a government agency (hence the top-level domain *gov*), its particular name is *nasa,* the particular computer where this service resides is named *gsfc* (whatever that means), and the service is particular to the World Wide Web (*www*). Electronic mail (email) addresses include the person's own user ID (quite often a first initial and last name: hkissinger, for example), followed by the @ sign (read *at*), and the particular domain name of the person's email account. The World Wide Web adds a different twist to domain names: the way in which the domain is to be accessed, followed by the characters ":// " followed by the domain name. This is called the site's URL, or Universal Resource Locator. For example, the URL http://www.gsfc.nasa.gov means access the site www.gsfc.nasa.gov using HyperText Transport Protocol (http). Common top-level domains include *edu* (an educational institution: harvard.edu), *com* (a commercial institution: aol.com), *net* (a network: city.net), and *org* (another kind of organization: nysernet.org). In all these examples, note the conventional lack of upper-case letters.

WHAT'S ON THE INTERNET

The Internet provides researchers with many tools. Communication media such as email, Usenet discussion groups and mailing lists (often called *listservs*) allow you to communicate with others in the world who have Internet access and to join academic (and sometimes not-so-academic) discussions with others in any area of interest. Information tools such as telnet, anonymous ftp, WAIS, Gopher, and the World Wide Web (often called "WWW" or simply "the Web") allow you to find and retrieve information stored on computers nearly anywhere in the world. Generally each of these tools has one or more search engines associated with it for finding and retrieving needed information.

Email

Description
If you've used the Internet at all, it has probably been with email—sending and receiving messages to and from friends and family. But email can benefit you as a researcher as well. More and more authorities (university and private researchers, journalists, government officials) use email. Many (not all, of course) may welcome an inquiry from a student and may very well respond with an informed and authoritative reply. Don't overlook the research potential of email. Through it you may conduct interviews and even exchange computer files not available to the general Internet user (text, graphics, charts, statistics, and so forth) with

persons who have such information to share. Occasionally a scholar will be willing to share with you a current draft of a new project or an unpublished conference paper.

Reliability
In a word, consider the source. If you're corresponding with a noted scholar, professor, researcher, or authority, you may quote (and cite) with some confidence. Otherwise, be wary. If you exchanged letters or had a phone conversation with this person, would it seem authoritative?

Accessing
How do you find email addresses of people with whom you'd like to correspond? Currently, the best answer to this question is simply to ask them. There are guides, directories, databases, and search engines for email, but unfortunately none of them work particularly well. The Internet needs a phone book, but there isn't one. You will find, however, that the email addresses of people who contribute to newsgroups and discussion lists are included in the header of the message they send. It's a good idea to keep a list of email addresses of people you may want to correspond with.

Usenet Discussion Groups (or Newsgroups)

Description
Newsgroups are the most problematic of the Internet categories. There are currently over 10,000 topical newsgroups. The easiest way to visualize a newsgroup is to think of a standard cork bulletin board hanging on a wall. Anyone can walk by and tack up a message, and anyone else can come by and read the message, respond to it, or put up a new message. Newsgroups on the Internet are electronic versions of those bulletin boards—anyone with an Internet account can use a newsreader to check out a continuing discussion, read the current messages, and post a reply or a new message. The discussions range from wild, sometimes nearly obscene, free-for-alls on controversial topics, complete with name-calling and other personal attacks (called *flaming*), to sane and civilized discussions, often by noted authorities, containing interesting and useful facts and intelligent, if cautious, speculation.

Reliability
Because newsgroups are a radically democratic forum in which everyone—the uninformed and the expert—has a voice, use information gleaned from this medium sparingly and with caution.

Accessing

Your school must subscribe to a newsfeed, a central computer where all the messages are stored and transferred to other providers. If so, you will have access to a newsreader of some kind and be able to choose which newsgroups to try to follow (remember, there are well over 10,000), and which messages to read. Newsgroups are grouped hierarchically, much as are domain names, in a series of units separated by dots. For example, the newsgroup rec.music.bluenote.blue is of type *recreation,* subtype *music,* particular category *bluenote,* and topic *blue* and is a discussion of blues music. Other types include *alt* (the alternative groups, often wild and uncensored); *comp* (computers); *K12* (for students in grades K through 12); *misc* (miscellaneous, not to be confused with alt.); *sci* (science); and *soc* (societies, countries, cultures). You will be able to reply to messages just as you can with email. Remember, however, that what you write in newsgroup posts is public.

Discussion Lists (or Listservs)

Description

Academic discussion lists are becoming the staple of serious academic researchers and others. They are similar to newsgroups, with one significant difference: you must actively subscribe to the list, and after doing so you receive the messages directly as individual email messages. The mailing of the discussions is essentially managed by automated computer programs that receive all incoming messages and immediately forward them to everyone who subscribes to the list; one of the most common of these automated programs is called Listserv, hence the generic (if technically incorrect) reference to discussion lists as listservs. While not exactly private, since anyone can subscribe to any discussion list, lists usually stick to their stated topics, are less prone to flaming, and are more likely to be frequented by serious and knowledgeable contributors.

Reliability

Though the potential for unreliable information exists on lists, it's less frequent than in newsgroups. In general, to assess the reliability of information, consider the author's credentials and authority.

Accessing

To find a listing of currently active academic listservs, use your WWW browser to access the URL http://www.mid.net/KOVACS/index.html (see below for accessing WWW sites). If you find one to which you'd like to subscribe, send an email message to the listserv (the machine that manages the list), not to the list itself. The message must contain the word *subscribe* followed by the name of the list to which you want to subscribe, followed by your first name, followed by your last name. The message must not contain anything else. For example, if your name is Mary Rose and you want to subscribe to the Distance Education list, send the message *subscribe deos-l Mary Rose* to the listserv's address. After you have subscribed, you will receive further instructions about using the list and posting to it.

Generally it's a good idea to *lurk* (i.e., read all the messages without contributing anything) for a few weeks, to ensure that you don't break any of the rules of *netiquette,* the unwritten rules of the particular culture of the list. Most lists have *FAQs* or frequently asked questions, a compilation of questions about the intent and operation of the list so those on the list don't have to answer the same questions repeatedly.

Many lists maintain archives of all their discussions; if you want to review what has been written on the list previously about a particular topic, you may search the archives. Instructions on how to do this are provided when you subscribe.

LURKING

Lurking refers to the practice of just reading, without responding to, the posts from a listserv or a newsgroup. Generally speaking, it's almost mandatory to lurk for two or three weeks to get the feel of a list or group. Violations of netiquette—posting inappropriate, off-topic messages, asking stupid questions, or generally not knowing the workings of the group —are often dealt with harshly on Usenet and listservs.

Telnet

Telnet is, strictly speaking, not a repository of facts and information, but a tool. It allows you to use your computer as a remote terminal to another computer. The drawback is that you usually need to have an account on the other computer as well. Some services—library catalogs, for instance—are available to the public through telnet. You may sit at your computer and telnet to the on-line catalog of a library in England, for example. Or, if you have access to an Internet account while traveling, you may telnet back to your own account at school and use it as if you were there.

Anonymous Ftp

Description

The abbreviation *ftp* stands for *File Transfer Protocol.* It's the standard method of transferring files (text documents, graphics, computer software, etc.) over the Internet. Normally, if you find a file you want to transfer to your own computer for viewing, you need to be able to access the computer where the information resides, in which case you would theoretically need an account on that computer and a password. However, many computer systems worldwide have been made at least partially accessible to "anonymous" users—people who don't have accounts. Hence, anonymous ftp provides a means for you to retrieve files from computers you normally wouldn't have access to.

Reliability

Information gathered through anonymous ftp is usually as reliable as print information in a library (e.g., government documents, research reports, and statistical tabulation of data). You may actually access visual and graphical information such as pictures from the Hubble Space Telescope, available from NASA.

Accessing

The search engine for ftp is called Archie, short for "archiver." Archie servers scan the Internet at regular intervals, looking for anonymous ftp sites and cataloging what they find. With Archie, you perform keyword searches for titles of files: you simply give Archie a filename (if you know it, and of course you don't) or a partial filename, and tell Archie to search its accumulated catalog looking for ftp sites containing files whose names include the string of letters you've supplied. (Boolean operators are limited to OR.) Once Archie finds all the sites, it lists them. The limitations of Archie are its inability to look for subjects or words *within* files, and that often filenames are not at all descriptive of their contents. After Archie finds a file, you then must begin the anonymous ftp process, instructing your computer to transfer the desired file from the remote computer where Archie has indicated it exists.

Using anonymous ftp from a text-based (command-line) account is a fairly complex procedure; it requires, as always, the knowledge of a number of arcane commands (or at least a good reference chart). Even then, retrieving files by ftp can be arduous. And remember, the files, after being retrieved, now reside in your account on your college's mainframe computer, not on the personal computer you're using. You must initiate a second transfer procedure—most likely using Kermit or Xmodem or Zmodem—to move the files to your own computer.

Fortunately, newer Internet tools such as Gopher and the WWW browser Lynx (discussed later) as well as graphical/PPP ftp applications such as Anarchie for the Macintosh can perform anonymous ftp simply and transparently.

WAIS

Description
WAIS stands for Wide Area Information Server. (It's pronounced "waze," by the way.) WAIS is an indexing package developed by Apple Computers Inc., Dow Jones, and Thinking Machines, Inc. It is a standard method of indexing large databases so they may be accessed by any computer over the Internet. WAIS is both an interface (a way of organizing and presenting data) and its own search engine. That is, finding and retrieving information with WAIS are one and the same operation.

Reliability
Much like the documents obtainable through anonymous ftp, WAIS-found documents tend to be substantial and trustworthy.

Accessing
You either need a WAIS program on your computer or you may telnet to one, such as that found at bbs.oit.unc.edu. Follow instructions, which will vary depending on the software you're using and the WAIS site you've accessed. You first need to do a keyword search to find the actual databases you want to search. Once you've located the databases, do a second keyword search to find the documents contained in the relevant databases.

Gopher

Description
Until the advent of the World Wide Web and its graphical interface browsers, Gopher had become the tool of choice for locating and retrieving information on the Internet. Though it was originally text-based, graphical Gopher clients are now available for both Macintosh and Windows. Gopher presents a pleasing and easy-to-use standardized menu interface, allowing you to make selections from a list of choices rather than memorizing and typing commands. Information is placed on Gopher servers, (specially configured computers), and Gopher clients access the information, presenting the available material to the user in the form of a menu of choices—a list of available documents which may be selected and displayed merely by manipulating a highlighter and pressing the enter key. Gopher has the further advantage of being able

to perform WAIS and ftp searches and retrievals, all in the background and unknown to the user, allowing it essentially to supersede the earlier WAIS and ftp modes.

Reliability
Owing to the enormous popularity of Gopher and its widespread use, Gopher is prone to turn up massive amounts of information, from archived listservs and newsgroups to valuable research documents. You must evaluate the material carefully.

Accessing
Gopher's search engine is called Veronica, and though Veronica sites worldwide are limited and very often you will get an "unable to connect" message because of high usage, it is simple to use. Using Gopher, you transfer to one of the Veronica sites and, when prompted, enter keywords. Veronica supports fairly complex boolean searches (see Chapter 2), so if you're interested in O. J. Simpson's football career but don't want to read hundreds of articles about the trial, for example, you can tell Veronica to find *O. J. Simpson* but exclude any article containing the word *trial.* After you initiate the search, Veronica presents you with a menu (up to twelve pages worth) of items containing the keywords you designated. To read any of them, select with the moving highlighter, using the arrow keys, and press enter. Gopher will retrieve the item and display it, if it's text. Gopher can find and retrieve non-text documents as well; it will ask if you'd like to download these, since it cannot display them. For text-based Gophers, remember that downloading means bringing to your college's mainframe, not to your own computer. (Some recent versions of the text-based Gopher can download directly to your PC, however.)

World Wide Web

Description
Currently the most popular way of browsing and searching the Internet is the World Wide Web. Its popularity derives both from its hypertext interface (clicking on the screen brings you to a new page of information) and its ability to display color and graphics. In addition, like its predecessor Gopher, the Web with its clients has subsumed all previous Internet modes: browsers can perform hypertext links (which is the underlying principle of the Web) but also can use Gopher, WAIS, and ftp.

Reliability
Surfing the Web is potentially the most treacherous of the information-gathering activities. Individuals, commercial operations, and organiza-

tions may create their own websites. So while you may find research reports, government documents, and on-line medical journals, you may also find unsubstantiated opinion, self-serving hype, and crazed propaganda from every radical splinter-group that's ever had its fifteen minutes of fame on the six o'clock news. Judge the material carefully.

Accessing

Information for the WWW is stored on specially configured computers called *webservers;* each particular document is called a *webpage* or just a page; a collection of pages is called a *website*. The principle of hypertext allows the user to explore the websites on the Internet in an intuitive manner: if you see something on the screen that you'd like to explore further and it's linked to more information, just click the mouse or press the appropriate key, and you're there. This allows for non-linear browsing (i.e., following associative leads to other documents rather than reading straight through from beginning to end).

Though the Web is accessible through a text-based browser known as Lynx, most likely you will be using a graphical browser such as Netscape. As you're viewing a document with Netscape, linked text (i.e., text that connects to another document) will usually be underlined and shown in blue; linked graphics are usually outlined in blue. Clicking the mouse on linked text or graphics will immediately take you to the connected document. If the trail you follow begins to seem fruitless, you can back out of it by clicking the mouse on the left-pointing arrow near the top of the Netscape screen. With enough backward steps like this, eventually you'll return to where you began, for a fresh start.

The Web has many different search engines, but all work on the keyword search principle. Some of the most popular are Webcrawler (http://webcrawler.com/), Yahoo (http://www.yahoo.com), and Infoseek (accessible by the Net Search button in Netscape.) One valuable site in Switzerland—W3 Search Engines—collects many of the most popular engines on one page and allows you to use any or all of them (http://cuiwww.unige.ch/meta-index.html).

EVALUATING SOURCES

The Internet versus Print Media

For centuries, the printed book and other forms of print media have ruled the storage and distribution of information, and those who controlled the media controlled the information and in some sense controlled the flow of information. *Controlled* may be too harsh a word here—not every author, publisher, editor, and encyclopedia-article writer has been obsessed with nefarious schemes to manipulate the minds of the people, and there have always been educators or other wise and informed people to warn of the danger of mindlessly believing everything you read. This attitude has, in recent years, come to be known as critical thinking, learning to question what you see, hear, and read before you decide whether or not to accept it.

For better or for worse (and it actually has been some of each), the print media and their built-in limitations have provided us with a filter for our information. Because publishing resources (materials, time, and effort necessary to write and revise) were relatively precious, only a small part of what humanity wanted to say could be printed. And somebody had to decide which part that would be. Presumably only the best, most useful and valuable, most interesting, and most worthy material was published. Thus, every day someone decided *not* to publish something.

There arose a special class of humanity: the writers. Some of us were writers; most of us were not. Authors, by their ability to compose and publish, had authority (the similarity of terms is not coincidental), knowledge, wisdom, and permanence for their ideas.

However, today, everyone is (or can be, disregarding issues of access for certain groups of people for the moment) an author electronically. It is, in some ways, the embodiment of democracy—no one's voice is silenced. But in this new cacophonous world, the sheer quantity and accessibility of information have intensified the need for critical thinking. We are awash in a sea of information; in fact, some of what surrounds us can't even be dignified with that term. There is, for example, a Usenet newsgroup devoted specifically to the writing of unkind words about Barney the Dinosaur.

Holy wars (i.e., arguments that are impossible to win and that go on interminably) surround us and are, if anything, encouraged by the anonymity of the faceless conversations that occur over the Net. We argue, in electronic print, about Islam versus Judaism, pro-life versus pro-choice, pro-environment versus pro-jobs, Macintosh versus Windows, about purple dinosaurs. And, like the worst of the TV talk shows, the arguments often degenerate into name-calling, false accusations, irrational thinking and speaking, rumors transmitted as fact, and pure and simple lies. All this arguing and flaming can be broadcast to literally tens of millions of people.

The town lunatic who used to sit on his porch muttering racial, ethnic, or sexual slurs was only heard by a few and was ignored or tolerated. Had he written a book, or even a letter to the local newspaper, his words never would have seen type. Now, if he has a computer and a modem, he can publish to the world.

The challenge to the serious researcher becomes apparent: how do you judge what's valid and useful and what's not? Who can you believe, when everyone is shouting at you? What criteria can you use?

Critically Examining Your Sources

In many ways the problem of knowing what to do with the information you gather from the Internet is as knotty a problem as finding the information in the first place. You already have some experience with evaluating print media to draw on, however, so you simply need to be more vigilant in applying your criteria, since now there's no publisher, editor, or review board of knowledgeable people in the field to do the evaluating and selecting for you. But the principles of critical thinking—whether applied to print media or visual media such as television or computer media—remain the same.

Critical Mindset

Critical thinking is, more than anything else, a habit of mind, a particular action you take almost reflexively when confronted with information. When using the Internet, it's crucial to question your information, to be a professional and committed Doubting Thomas. Assume, at the beginning, that anything you read is *not true*. Demand evidence or support from your sources. In the more interactive parts of the Internet—Usenet and listservs especially—you have the opportunity to question in person. For material that's not "live" and offers no interactivity, you must question your sources virtually, silently and often alone. (By the way, never hesitate to try out an idea on a friend, a colleague, a roommate, someone whose judgment you trust. That's just good writing advice and sound academic procedure.)

Try to imagine *what if . . . ?* or *what about . . . ?* scenarios, counter examples which may disprove or at least call into question what you're reading. If someone writes, "it's acceptable to sacrifice the spotted owls because otherwise a lot of humans will be out of work, and suffering," ask yourself, "but what if there weren't any spotted owls?" And vice versa. If someone writes, "Robber barons such as Andrew Carnegie are examples of the failure of capitalism," ask, "What about the tens of millions of dollars Carnegie gave to charities?" Make this kind of thinking automatic.

Probably the hardest part of critically examining a source or an idea is dealing with information you already know or believe, or perhaps simply want to believe. If you're a life-long Democrat, it may be difficult to be critical of statements of Democratic principles. But it's just as crucial, maybe even more crucial, to do so. Your argument, your reasoning, your judgment, and ultimately your writing will be more convincing if you've carefully examined and critiqued your ideas, even your most deeply held ideas, and can show your readers that you've thought this problem through.

Repeat this mantra: nothing on the Internet is true; nothing on the Internet is true; nothing on the Internet. . . .

Who Are You?

Part of evaluating your sources and your information is your sense of self, of who you are, and how you want to appear in your research writing. If you want to appear calm and scientific and detached, choose evidence that makes you look that way. If you want to appear more passionate and committed, chose that kind of evidence.

Specificity

One of the marks of a believable source is specificity—actual content, facts, figures, statistics, and research conducted or cited. If someone writes, "Most of the people who use the Internet are men," you may or may not be inclined to believe it, but you probably won't be swayed. But if someone writes, "Recent studies of Internet users show that 78% are male, 90% are white, and 77% make over $60,000 per year," it sounds more convincing, and can probably be verified by referring to recent studies. But don't drop your critical guard—statistics can be misused, exaggerated, and even entirely fabricated (as those above are).

Audience

As in any writing project, you must know your audience well. You must consider what those who will be reading your research paper will accept as proof and authoritative commentary. If your audience will expect you to present lots of facts and figures, then find facts and figures. If your audience is likely to strongly disagree with you, you need strong and irrefutable evidence. If your audience is novices in the field about which you are writing, you need more accessible, easily visualized, and striking information. If your audience is other experts in the field, you need more precise and specialized information to make your case.

Knowledge of Speaker

How much do you know about the speaker/writer? Particularly in listservs and Usenet newsgroups, it's possible to follow along for a few weeks and note who the frequent posters (a message sent to the list or newsgroup is called a *post*) are and, more importantly, how authoritative they seem. Do they consistently know what they're talking about? Do other posters on the list recognize them as knowledgeable? Or, on the other hand, does the poster have a history of flaming, of irrational and unjustifiable statements?

In Internet modes other than listservs and Usenet, it's more difficult to evaluate a source. Sometimes you can search in one of the engines for an author's or an organization's name, and track down other works. This will allow you to get a fuller picture of authors, what they stand for, and what kinds of biases or prejudices they exhibit.

A Sense of the Writer's Authority

The writer's authority is not the same as what you know or can discover explicitly about the source. Instead it's a subjective feeling you have, based on the author's tone, grasp of the language, and conventions of the field. Most people can sense this in face-to-face encounters; very often on meeting someone for the first time, you get an indefinable feeling about the person's competence. It takes a little more cultivation, but you can develop the same sense about someone's writing. If you have instincts about a source, trust them until they are proven incorrect.

Verifiability

Much of what you read on the Internet will be unverifiable, in the scientific sense of the word. You won't be able to reproduce experiments, find the ultimate source of information, or check out material presented as fact. In some instances you will, however. Some information on the Net resembles pure academic discourse, complete with footnotes and a bibliography. While other material ranges from flaming to carefully considered opinion.

Other Points of View

A critical thinker constantly seeks other points of view. They are necessary to help develop thinking skills.

Fortunately, the Internet will often force an overwhelming multiplicity of views upon you, and if you seem to be receiving only one side of a story, it's a simple matter to find opposing points of view. When you are confronted with overwhelming amounts of information on practically any subject, both sides (or all twenty-five sides) will be represented somewhere.

In the narrowly-focused Usenet groups, often you won't find opposing viewpoints represented—the nature and purpose of newsgroups is to let people focus discussion on a particular topic. While posters to the newsgroup rec.music.bluenote.blues may argue, for example, about whether Eric Clapton is or is not a great blues guitarist, you won't find anyone praising Bach. And if anyone did, it would be a breach of netiquette; the poster could be driven out of the newsgroup either by being flamed, humiliated, gently reminded that he's in the wrong group, or ignored.

Usenet and listserv postings follow *threads*—sequences of postings on the same topic, each one responding to the previous message or perhaps introducing a new perspective. This is the beauty of newsgroups and lists, and it makes critical thinking necessary. In fact, taken as a whole, a thread is critical thinking embodied. If you follow a thread over a period of a week or so (most don't last much longer than a week, burning out as participants move on to new discussions), you will be tossed to and fro, intellectually, as each new posting brings a new idea, a new perspective, a new *what if . . . ?* or *have you considered . . . ?*

In the less interactive modes of the Net (i.e., repositories of more or less unchanging information on ftp sites and gophersites and websites), opposing points of view don't automatically appear. But you can search for them. You just need to remember to do so. Most Web search engines provide brief summaries of the contents of sites found while searching, so it's easy to tell at a glance if you've found conflicting information. With ftp sites and gophersites, you'll have to retrieve the information and examine each document individually, since ftp and Gopher searches retrieve nothing more than names of sites, folders, or documents.

MOVING INFORMATION OVER THE NET

TCP/IP is the set of rules that explain how computers can talk to each other over the Internet. These rules are necessarily complicated and rigid, since computers cannot think. If computer B doesn't understand the pulses of electricity coming from computer A, then there's no communication. It's like sending messages in Morse code to someone who doesn't have any idea what the code is.

So there are standards, one of which is ASCII text, the standard that says if I press the *k* key on my Macintosh, your IBM will read it as a *k* as well. This is fine for text, and it's why text transfers over the Internet are so easy and efficient. It's just sending 128 alphanumeric characters (letters, numbers, and some punctuation marks) between two machines that use exactly the same codes. But pictures, sound, and word-processor formattings—so-called binary files—are not standardized between differ-ent computers and systems, which creates a big problem.

Additionally, with the growth of complexity and power in comput-ing, file sizes seem to be increasing. Huge files of 10 megabytes (10 mil-lion characters, 80 million ones and zeros) are common, and computers, modems, and phone lines just cannot handle that amount of informa-tion quickly and efficiently. So, along with speeding up computers, mak-ing faster modems, and improving phone line quality worldwide, other methods of speeding file transfers are needed.

The solution to both problems—files of more than plain text, and very large files—is achieved partly through the *translation* of the files. Non-text binary files are usually, but not always, converted into text files through a process called encoding, which makes them roughly one-seventh larger. Large files then undergo a transformation called compression—squeezing the files to make them smaller to send. When they are received, they need to be "unsqueezed," that is, decompressed to their full size. Unfortunately, there is no standard for either binary encoding or compression. Different computer systems use different methods, and even within computer systems there are different methods.

One convention that is almost standard is that of indicating encoding and compression routines with filename extensions—three- or four-letter markers added to the end of a filename after a period, to indicate the file-type(s). You're probably familiar with the extension *.txt* meaning text file. Extensions can be piled up, one on the other. It's quite common for a file to be first compressed (which makes it a binary file) and then encoded to an ASCII text file for sending over the Internet. Both operations will leave their extensions on the filename, e.g., *clintonpicture.sit.hqx,* which means that the original filename is *clintonpicture,* the file has been compressed using the Macintosh compression utility Stuffit (.sit), and then that com-pressed binary file has been converted into a text file with the routine *bin-hex* (.hqx—don't ask about the logic of the extension abbreviations) for sending over the Internet.

Fortunately, since the number of compression and encoding schemes is limited, a few mega-utilities are being developed which can uncompress, unencode, and read almost any of the main translation rou-tines used by the major computer systems. But you still need a small repertoire of file-conversion software utilities on your own computer for handling the files you're likely to get as you scour the Internet. Fortu-nately, most are free or shareware, and are easily available on the major commercial services and via ftp, Gopher, or the World Wide Web. Major conversion schemes and the type of computer system associated with each are listed in Table 1.1.

TABLE 1.1   Conversion Schemes

File Extension	Type of Computer System	Purpose
.z	UNIX	Compression
.Z	UNIX	Compression
.tar	UNIX	Multiple file archives
.bin	Macintosh	Binary encoding
.cpt	Macintosh	Compression
.hqx	Macintosh	ASCII-encoded binary
.sea	Macintosh	Compression
.sit	Macintosh	Compression
.arc	PC	Compression
.arj	PC	Compression
.lzh	PC	Compression
.pak	PC	Compression
.voc	PC	Sound
.wav	PC	Sound
.zip	PC	Compression
.zoo	PC	Compression
.GIF	Universal	Binary graphic format
.jpeg	Universal	Binary graphic format
.ps	Universal	ASCII (Postscript)

CHANGE ON THE INTERNET

The Internet is an amazingly dynamic medium. It is estimated to be growing by 100 percent every ten months. In addition, sites of information and the information itself change constantly. If you find information in one place one day, don't be surprised if the next day you return to that site and find the information changed or gone. In fact, the site itself may be gone.

As with taking notes from printed sources, be sure you get the necessary information to cite your source. Copy it down by hand, or cut and paste the URLs into a special file you keep open on your computer—whatever it takes to get that information.

FINAL WORDS

While you may find that the World Wide Web is the easiest and most interesting way to find information on the Internet, don't overlook ftp, WAIS, and Gopher. These are more than just different ways of looking at the Internet. Often they contain different documents and different information, so it's best to conduct an Archie and a Veronica search, as well as checking out a few different WWW search engines, such as AltaVista, Yahoo, and Infoseek.

2

BOOLEAN LOGIC

Boolean logic is a branch of mathematics invented by the 19th century mathematician George Boole. Boole was interested in finding mathematically precise ways of describing logical thought, and he developed a theory of classes and sets (collections) that has become useful in the twentieth century both for designing computers and for using them. This mathematical model is called boolean algebra or boolean logic. It has become very important recently as the size of information collections has increased. On the Internet, boolean logic has become a useful way of delimiting information.

Boolean logic uses a syntax that employs the operators AND, OR and NOT to describe sets or collections of items. For example, if you were looking for a collection of monarchs, you would accept either references to kings *or* references to queens. In boolean terms, that set could then be described by the phrase *king OR queen.* (By convention, the boolean operators AND, OR, and NOT are always written in all capital letters.) The OR operator has the effect of expanding the set of items you're describing, because it allows more than one class.

By contrast, if you wanted to describe a set of items each of which has the characteristics of being a restaurant and being Chinese, you would use the phrase *Chinese AND restaurant.* This is the intersection of two sets or classes of items—all things Chinese and all restaurants. If an item belongs to both sets—that is, if it's both a restaurant and Chinese—then it's a part of the set you've described. The AND operator serves to limit a class by requiring each item in the set to have multiple characteristics; any item that has only one characteristic (such as any old restaurant) is not part of the set.

The boolean operator NOT allows you to describe sets that exclude a certain class of items. For example, if you wanted to describe the set of medieval English writers other than Chaucer, you would use the boolean phrase *medieval NOT Chaucer*.

Actually, in the preceding example, you are describing a set much larger than the one you actually want, for the class *medieval* can include churches and knights and festivals, as well as French and Icelandic items. So you would use a more complex boolean phrase to ensure that only medieval English writers are included and Chaucer is excluded. That phrase would be *medieval AND English AND writers NOT Chaucer*. Descriptors can be strung together in strings longer than two, using multiple combinations of class-words (e.g., English) and operators.

To take the example a couple of steps further, you could consider that either the word *English* or the word *British* is used to describe things pertaining to the isle and its empire. So the word *English* could be replaced by the unit *(English OR British)*. Here the parentheses are used to indicate the *nesting* function. Nesting means that the items within the parentheses should be taken as a unit. In the preceding phrase, *writers* could be replaced by the nested unit *(writers OR authors)* as well, since either the word *writer* or the word *author* may be used to describe people who compose words on paper (or on the computer screen!).

So the most precise description, using boolean terms, for the medieval English writers other than Chaucer would be *medieval AND (English OR British) AND (writers OR authors) NOT Chaucer*.

VENN DIAGRAMS

Sometimes a visual representation of boolean phrases may be used to illustrate the set being described. These diagrams, usually interlocked circles, are called *Venn diagrams,* after their inventor, the English logician and mathematician John Venn (1834–1923).

Imagine that the class of all royal females who've ruled a country (i.e, queens), can be represented in the abstract by a circle containing all queens, as in Figure 2.1. Now imagine the class of all royal males who've ruled a country can be represented by another circle—kings—such as the one in Figure 2.2. It's easy to visualize, then, that the boolean phrase *queens OR kings* can be represented by the dark parts of Figure 2.3. In this Venn diagram, everything in dark, i.e., all of both circles, represents the boolean construction *queens OR kings*. Everyone who has been either a king or queen falls somewhere in the dark region. Notice that the two dark circles do not overlap at all—no one can be both a king AND queen simultaneously, so there is no representation for the empty category *kings AND queens.*

Now, refer to Figure 2.1 again which shows the category of queens. In addition, the class *people named Elizabeth* is shown in Figure 2.4. Now, the intersection, or *overlap,* of these two classes—*queens* and *people named Elizabeth*—is what we mean by the boolean phrase *queens AND people named Elizabeth.* In Figure 2.5, the category of *Queen Elizabeths*—the category of people who belong to both the class *Elizabeth* and the class *queens* at the same time—is represented by the dark section. Notice that

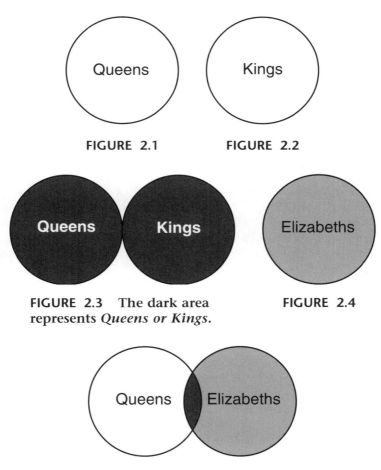

FIGURE 2.1   **FIGURE 2.2**

FIGURE 2.3   **The dark area represents *Queens or Kings.***   **FIGURE 2.4**

FIGURE 2.5   **The dark area represents *Queens AND Elizabeths.***

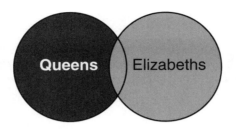

FIGURE 2.6   The dark area
represents *Queens NOT Elizabeth.*

this dark section is much smaller than either category alone—the AND operator is a way of restricting or limiting categories.

Now for the final boolean operator, NOT. Imagine you wanted to describe, in boolean terms, the category of *all the queens besides the Elizabeths.* The boolean phrase would be *queens NOT Elizabeth.* This category would be represented by the dark area of the Venn diagram in Figure 2.6. From this diagram, you can see that all members belonging to both the class *queens* and the class *Elizabeths* at the same time have been excluded from the category described by *queens NOT Elizabeth.*

Venn diagrams can be constructed, in theory at least, to illustrate even the most complicated boolean phrases. Even the phrase *medieval AND (English OR British) AND (writers OR authors) NOT Chaucer* can be represented by a series of interlocking figures and shadings, but the figure would be so complicated that its use as a visualization tool would be limited.

BOOLEAN LOGIC AND SEARCHING THE INTERNET

What's the value of this excursion into the abstract realm of boolean mathematics? You will see in the next chapter that finding anything on the Internet requires being able to describe exactly what you're looking for. Since computers can't read your mind or understand natural languages like English or Spanish or Tagalog, you need a way to describe the set or collection of information you want so the computer can go out onto the Internet and find it for you.

Normally what this means is that you find a program that's able to search the Internet—these programs are called *search engines.* The way you communicate with search engines is through boolean phrases (and other boolean-like phrases, which extend the capabilities of the three basic boolean operators) called *queries*. The search engine provides you with a place (a *query box*) to type your carefully-constructed query, and it then scours the Internet looking for information that fits the category you've described. Hence, an understanding of boolean logic is the first step in being able to tell a search engine what to find for you.

EXERCISES

1. What are the three boolean operators?

2. Explain in your own words how the AND operator limits a category and the OR operator expands a category.

3. Compose a boolean phrase that describes the set of pies that are either apple or peach.

4. Is the boolean phrase *(coffee AND cream) OR sugar* the same as *coffee AND (cream OR sugar)*? Why or why not?

5. Draw a Venn diagram for both phrases in question 4.

3

SEARCHING THE INTERNET

The Internet is a huge repository of information both static and dynamic. It has been likened to many different ideas: a fire hose of information (when you only want a sip), a refrigerator door covered with messages from everyone, a haystack (when you want the needle), and, of course, the best-known of all, an information superhighway.

But if it's the world's largest highway system, there's no roadmap. It's the world's largest cable TV system, and there's no *TV Guide*. It's bigger than the phone system, and there's no phone book (actually, there is a book called the *Internet Yellow Pages*, but it's not what you'd expect). It's the world's biggest book, with tens of billions of words, and there's no table of contents or index.

It's probably most helpful, however, to liken it to something with which you're already familiar—a library. To use this analogy to understand the joys and frustrations of searching the Net, we can say there's an unimaginable amount of information stored in this virtual library, you can obtain it and check it out instantly, but unfortunately there's no card catalog.

What you do have to help you as you try to find information on the Internet are search engines.

SEARCH ENGINES

Search engine is the term applied to the various computer programs that allow you to look for and retrieve information throughout the Internet. These are usually free, easily accessible, and fairly effective—if you know how to use them. Each has its own quirks, and its own strengths and weaknesses.

Each of the major modes of the Internet has its own search engines, though as is common in the evolution of the Internet, the more recent technologies tend to subsume the earlier technologies. The World Wide Web browsers (see Chapter 5) can browse the Web, but they also can perform Gopher and ftp operations (see Chapter 6). Gopher, on the other hand, cannot perform Web operations. Searching Usenet and listserv archives is the most complex, because the technology is still primitive (in Internet terms, anyway). To search ftp sites, you use the engine known as Archie. (short for "archiver") To search gopherspace, you have two options: Veronica and Jughead (after Archie, the metaphors become silly). WAIS is WAIS—it is its own search engine. And the current focus of all the excitement about the Internet, the World Wide Web, has the largest variety of search engines, with such intriguing names as Yahoo, WebCrawler, WWWWorm, Excite, and Lycos.

Essentially a search engine allows you to type a description of what you're looking for into a query box, sometimes accompanied by commands to instruct the search engine what to do with your description and what kind of description it is. The general process is the same for all the search engines: describe what you're looking for, in terms that the search engine can understand, and wait for the results to come back to you.

There are two models of search engines: spiders and directories. Actually, many purists object to calling directories search engines, since in a true directory you browse, hoping to find useful information much as you would if you were to go to a particular section of your library and wander up and down the stacks, looking for something interesting. But most of the directories also allow you to input search descriptions and

---

BROWSING VS. SEARCHING

Browsing and Searching are the two ways of locating and retrieving information from the Internet. Browsing refers to examining hierarchically-arranged lists, usually called directories, and following leads to more directories that look interesting, until you eventually come to a list of sites where useful information may be stored. Searching refers to actively seeking out specific information that you can describe. Browse when you're not exactly sure of what information you want or expect to find; search when you know exactly what you want.

search a particular directory, so the distinction is blurred. In practice, most people refer to both as search engines.

Most of the search engines for the World Wide Web, as well as Archie and Veronica, use the spider model: at specified intervals, automated robot programs crawl over all the websites they know, gathering information on the contents of the sites, following links to other sites, and generally branching out to cover as much of the Internet as they can. They then index the titles, the words, and the contents for each site they have visited, and thereby maintain a comprehensive database of what's on the Net at that moment. When you initiate a search in one of the spider-based engines (WebCrawler, AltaVista, Lycos, Excite, etc.) you are essentially searching the database that's been gathered and stored on the engine's home computer. This prevents tying up the Web with millions of searches every minute.

Directories, on the other hand, arrange their sites into hierarchical categories. The sites included in directories are ones that have been registered by their owners, and (at least in most cases) not ones that the spider has found on its regular excursions over the Internet. This has the effect of limiting the sites included, but also biases the results toward the more aggressively-managed sites, particularly those with commercial interest or support. Recently a number of directory-based engines have begun selecting sites on the basis of popularity, using various formulas for determining how popular a site is; once a site's popularity drops excessively, it is removed from the directory or dropped in precedence.

For example, the first and the best-known of the WWW directories, Yahoo, organizes its sites into fourteen categories: arts, business and economy, computers, education, and so forth. Within each category are subcategories, like branches. Within arts, for example, are the subcategories humanities, photography, architecture, and others. Choosing a subcategory from a list of choices might call up another list of menus or, depending on the depth of the category, a list of sites which you can explore without knowing precisely what you're looking for. This allows for pure browsing, moving to a category of sites you think may have information you need and simply snooping around to see what's available. Browsing through directories is not a particularly efficient method of finding information, but often it helps you get started on a topic that's relatively unknown to you.

KEYWORD SEARCHING

One of the most valuable (and important) skills for searching the Internet is the keyword search. Since computers don't understand English or any other natural language, telling one how to find what you're looking for is both an art and a skill, requiring knowledge, experience, and inventiveness. Most search engines operate on a variation of the *keyword search* principle: give it some words—keywords—that you associate with the topic you're researching, and it finds documents that are in some way associated with those keywords. You're familiar with this type of searching already: when you do a subject-heading search in your library's card catalog or in the *Reader's Guide to Periodical Literature,* or even when you look up a business in the Yellow Pages, you're doing a very simple keyword search. If you're interested in subscribing to some daily reading material, you look in the Yellow Pages under *newspapers.* That's a keyword. If you're looking for computers, you look under *computers;* if you're looking for attorneys, you look under *attorneys;* if you're looking for doctors, you look under *physicians* (surprise!). Finding the right keywords often means the difference between a successful search and an unsuccessful one. A single keyword that's too general will find too much information, one that's too narrow will not find enough information, and the wrong one (or one different from the one the search engine expects) may not find anything at all.

But of course searching the Internet is much more complex than looking up something in the Yellow Pages or a card catalog, so it calls for more complex ways of describing the information you're looking for. Each search engine has ways of constructing *queries,* carefully worded phrases or set of keywords that allow you to define more precisely the nature of the information you want. In large cities, the *restaurants* category in the Yellow Pages may run on for twenty or thirty or more pages of tiny type. Imagine if you're looking for Chinese restaurants near your home with meals under $10. You have to browse through literally thousands of listings, and then you may not recognize the address or be able to figure out if it's expensive or not. You'd like to be able to construct a query of the Yellow Pages, saying in effect "find me Chinese restaurants, near my house, with entrees under $10." Most Internet search engines allow you to do something like this.

QUERY

A query is a string of words, a phrase, that describes the set of information you're looking for, using boolean and quasi-boolean operators. It must conform to the query-construction rules of the particular engine you happen to be using.

However, because each search engine has its own peculiarities, you must pay attention to the characteristics of the one you happen to be using. First, which boolean operators does it offer to allow you to construct your queries, and which operator is its default? (That is, how does it search if you give it no additional instructions? If you ask it to search for *Chicano literature* does it find all documents containing *Chicano* as well as all documents containing *literature,* or only documents that contain both words?); Second, does it allow substring and wildcard searches? (That is, can you enter *Engl* or perhaps *Engl** and find documents with the words *England, England's,* and *English*?) Third, exactly what information does it scan when you enter your search—the whole text of every document, the titles of every document, or a list of keywords supplied by the author? Also, although there are a few exceptions, nearly all search engines ignore case, so it's immaterial whether you enter *gloria steinem, Gloria Steinem,* or even *gLoriA steiNEM,* for that matter. All of these concepts will be explored more fully in the following sections.

BOOLEAN LOGIC AND THE QUERY

Recall boolean logic from the preceding chapter. Boolean logic allows you to describe sets of information using class-words and the three operators AND, OR, and NOT. Since the Internet search engines contain (in most cases) all the words in every document they index, when you use a keyword to describe a class (in the true boolean sense), what you're really saying is find the *set of all documents containing this word.* (Be aware that in some instances, certain engines may only catalog titles or main headings or some other subset of all the words in a document.) For example, the query *fruit NOT apple* describes the set of all documents containing the word *fruit,* except those that also contain the word *apple.*

Most search engines today allow you to construct fairly elaborate queries using the three main boolean operators. If your search engine allows boolean operations, you could enter the keywords *Queen AND Elizabeth NOT ship.* This search would describe a set of information that contains both the words *Queen* and *Elizabeth,* but would take the additional step of excluding any of those that contain the word *ship,* allowing you to concentrate on the Queen herself but not be burdened with material about the ship named after her. In addition, some search engines allow *adjacency* operators (not true boolean operators but operating under similar principles). These might allow you to indicate, for example, that *St. Petersburg* must be taken as a phrase and that *St.* and *Petersburg* are not to be returned to you unless they occur as consecutive words.

Or, for another example, if you're looking for articles on Taiwan, you might also remember that it was formerly called Formosa, and to find all references to the island you would want to find articles that mentioned either Taiwan or Formosa. Using the boolean phrase *Taiwan OR Formosa* would describe the set of articles you're looking for and give you the broadest possible listing—the OR operator includes all references to any of the keywords you've entered.

Boolean operations provide the basis for constructing queries that are understandable by the various search engines and help you to find exactly what you're looking for.

OTHER (NON-BOOLEAN) LOGICAL OPERATORS

Sometimes those three little words AND, OR, and NOT are not adequate for constructing a query effectively. In these cases, the construction of queries may be enhanced with other logical operators, not all of which are true boolean operators but are often used by search engines nevertheless. These operators are:

- parentheses
- adjacency operators
- proximity operators
- string delimiters

Parentheses allow you to group (nest) certain phrases and force the engine to deal with your keywords in a certain order. Normally, search engines read strictly left to right. The boolean phrase *St. AND Martin OR Maarten* describes a set of information which contains the phrase *St. Martin* as well as the word *Maarten,* even if the Maarten is unaccompanied by a *St.* What you really want, probably, is a listing of documents which contain the keyword *St.* followed by either *Martin* or *Maarten;* the correct phrase would then be *St. AND (Martin OR Maarten).* This forces the search engine to find all documents containing either *Martin* or *Maarten* first, and then to limit those to ones which contain *St.* as well.

Less common, in fact restricted to only a few of the most sophisticated search engines, are the adjacency and proximity operators. The adjacency operator forces the search engine to consider adjacent keywords as a single unit. Often, a space between words indicates the boolean OR; the boolean phrase *Boston Red Sox* very likely is equivalent to *Boston OR Red OR Sox.* Entering such a phrase would turn up all references to Boston (the tea party, the Pops, baked beans, etc.), plus all references to red (Simply, Smith, October, white and blue, etc.), plus all references to Sox

(Chicago White, etc.). Instead, you need a way to indicate that the phrase *Boston Red Sox* is a unit. Some search engines indicate this with the ADJ operator: *Boston ADJ Red ADJ Sox;* others enclose the whole phrase in double quotation marks to indicate adjacency: *"Boston Red Sox."*

Finally, a less commonly used operator is the proximity operator. It tells the engine to return "hits" on documents in which the specified keywords occur within a designated number of words of each other, say fifty. This particular operator has fewer uses; use it to find sets of words that often occur together but not necessarily in sequence.

Some search engines allow you to search for parts of words, called *strings* (short for string of characters). Thus if you were searching for articles concerning England, you would conceivably want to find documents with *English* as well. So you would search for the string *Engl;* sometimes this is accomplished by indicating that the documents contain the keyword or sometimes a wild card character (usually the *), indicating that it doesn't matter which letters, if any, follow the designated string, as long as that particular string of letters is contained.

How an Engine Reads Queries

When you construct a query that's more than one word, the search engine first has to read your query. How does it do that? It uses a process called *parsing,* taking the keywords and phrases in a strict left to right order, and associating the logicals with the keyword that follows each one. The engine maintains in its virtual brain a temporary working set of items as it parses, working with one keyword at a time. This may seem logical—so intuitive that it's obvious and not worth mentioning.

But let's look carefully at the implications. In two-keyword strictly boolean searches, the order of the keywords is immaterial; *chocolate OR vanilla* will return the same set of documents as will *vanilla OR chocolate*. You can conceptualize the parsing process this way: the engine searches its database for all documents containing the word *chocolate* and makes a temporary list of them; then it scans its whole database again looking for documents containing the word *vanilla*. It adds the two lists together and gives you one long set. (This description is only metaphorical; it's not exactly what happens, mathematically speaking. It also assumes that there is no sorting of the sets going on and no limit to the length of the set; in fact, most engines do arrange their returned sets by some kind of ranking scheme and most cut off their sets after a certain number of items, whether it's 100 or 20,000.)

A two-word AND query is also reversible. Using the query *spiders AND snakes* will return (again, in theory) exactly the same set of items as will the query *snakes AND spiders*. Why? The engine searches its database

---

SUMMARY OF QUERY OPERATORS

Boolean

AND   Forces both keywords to appear in found set
OR   Allows any single keyword to appear in found set
NOT   Excludes keyword from found set
(. . .)   Groups keywords to change the order of parsing

Quasi-Boolean

ADJ   Forces keywords to appear in sequence; whole phrase operator
NEAR   Forces keywords to appear within a specified proximity
Substring/Wildcard   Finds various alternative forms of keywords

---

for all items containing the word *spiders*, and again makes a temporary list. Then, it scans that temporary list of items containing *spiders,* searching for just those items that contain the word *snakes* as well, and throwing out the ones that don't contain *snakes*. That's the set of items it presents to you—a list of documents which contain both the word *spiders* and the word *snakes*. Reversing the terms would not change the results. (In theory, one supposes, the query *NOT cream AND ice* would return the same set as *ice NOT cream,* but who would ever think to construct that kind of query? Actually, some search engines won't allow a query to begin with an operator.)

It starts to get tricky with more complex queries containing three or more keywords or non-boolean logicals such as the adjacency operator. Suppose you're interested in precious metals, and you want information on the current value of both gold and silver. So you construct the query *value AND gold OR silver*. Let's parse this query the way a search engine would and see what the results might be. First, it looks for all items containing the keyword *value*, then it remembers all those and searches that set of items containing *value* looking for items which now also contain the keyword *gold*. The current set it's working with is items containing both *value* and *gold*. Now, still remembering the set it's working with, it returns to its whole database (that's what OR means) and searches for items containing *silver*. Then it combines its two found sets and gives you one long list which contains two sets of items: the set containing both the words *value* and *gold,* and the set containing *silver*. Most likely, this is not what you wanted.

There are two ways around this: if the search engine allows some kind of grouping function (usually parentheses), you can group items and force the engine to parse the groups first; or usually (not always, however) you can manually rearrange your query so that keywords are parsed in the correct order. In this case, using either *value AND (gold OR silver)* or *gold OR silver AND value* would do it for you by forcing a search engine to operate on *gold OR silver* first, and then search that found set for all items containing *value*.

RANKING THE HITS

Some of the more sophisticated search engines will actually make an attempt to determine for you which of the hundreds or thousands of items found are most relevant to you. Of course they can't read your mind and know exactly which ones you'll want to use, but they can make guesses by using complex mathematical computations based on a variety of factors, such as whether your keywords appear near the beginning of the document, appear in the title of the document, or appear many times. These and more are computed by the search engine and determine a document's rank. This is a useful feature, because the most potentially useful documents appear first, saving you the trouble of perusing all 200 or 1,000 documents found. But remember, it's only a computer performing an abstract mathematical calculation—be skeptical of the rankings; take the trouble to scan some of the lower-ranked hits, just to be sure it's not devaluing a document that you really need. The search engine doesn't really *know* what's most relevant.

CONSTRUCTING EFFECTIVE QUERIES

The key (no pun intended) to constructing effective queries is to find the appropriate keywords and then effectively manipulate the logical operators accepted by the specific search engine you're using. But perhaps even more important is to revise and refine your search.

To construct your initial query, access your first search engine. Note which operators are provided. What are its defaults—an AND search treating entered keywords as strings, or an OR search on whole words? Then, consider the following points:

- What is my topic?
- What are the most important words I associate with my topic?
- Are there any groups of words that must be treated as a phrase unit?
- Can I anticipate any systematic irrelevancies that I may want to exclude at this time? (Don't worry too much here—you will find out soon enough if you're uncovering irrelevant information.)

A Sample Search Using AltaVista's Simple Query

AltaVista is one of the more popular search engines used on the World Wide Web. It will be discussed in more detail in Chapter 5, but at this point we're going to use it in a sample search to illustrate the process of constructing and refining a query.

First, even in its simple query mode, AltaVista offers a number of operators for constructing a fairly sophisticated query. Its default is a boolean OR (actually it's what's called a *fuzzy AND*—a combination of an AND and an OR search, with the results, if any, of the AND search given higher precedence than the results of the OR search). It offers the operators AND (which can be forced by the use of +), a forced phrase (indicated in AltaVista by either capitalizing consecutive words—*New York*—or enclosing consecutive words in double quotes—*"new york"*), the boolean NOT (indicated by -), and string or wildcard searches (indicated by *).

Say your topic, still fairly general at this point in your process, is endangered species. Let's see what AltaVista comes up with. Enter *endangered species* into AltaVista's query box (see Figure 3.1) and click on the Submit button to send your query to AltaVista for processing.

After you do this, AltaVista will spend a second or two processing your request, and return to you the screen shown in Figure 3.2.

Notice what this screen tells you: AltaVista found 116,278 instances of the word *endangered* and 749,727 instances of *species*. The first ten sites from its list are available for display; this list potentially contains "about 60000" webpages meeting your criteria. The first page found, *Supreme Court Decides Sweet Home Endangered Species Case,* is 3 K (Kilobytes) in size—a relatively small page—and it's dated March 19, 1996. The first few lines of the page are also shown, giving you some indication of what the page may be about. Since this is the World Wide Web, if you want to examine the page itself, you need only to click on the underlined title of the page and the page will appear.

Scroll down to the bottom of this screen, shown in Figure 3.3, and see the rest of the result of your search. From the row of digits 1–20 plus *[Next]* across the bottom of this page, you can infer that there are twenty screens total. (In fact, that's all AltaVista will show you—the first 200 webpages ranked according to their relevance. There is no way, short of refining your search, to gain access to the remaining 59,800 sites.) You can step through the results page by page, up to the twenty-page limit, by clicking on *[Next];* clicking on any particular number will take you to that specific page. But with 60,000 hits, your search has been too scattered, and the 200 hits you're able to see may not be particularly useful to you.

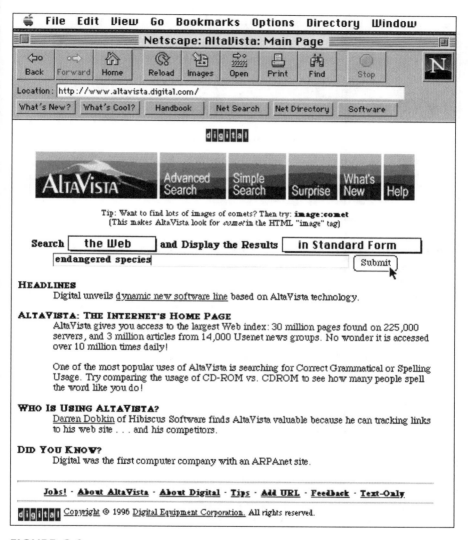

FIGURE 3.1

REFINING YOUR QUERIES

In this case, as is common, the result of your first query surprises and dis-
concerts you. You need to redo your query, called refining. There are
times when your query will turn up no sites, or only a few that aren't

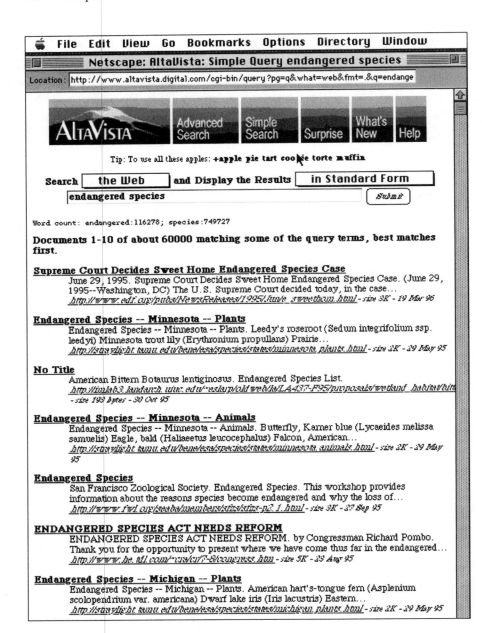

FIGURE 3.2

```
   File   Edit   View   Go   Bookmarks   Options   Directory   Window
```

Netscape: AltaVista: Simple Query endangered species

Location: http://www.altavista.digital.com/cgi-bin/query?pg=q&what=web&fmt=.&q=endange

June 29, 1995. Supreme Court Decides Sweet Home Endangered Species Case. (June 29, 1995--Washington, DC) The U.S. Supreme Court decided today, in the case...
http://www.edf.org/pubs/NewsReleases/1995/Jun/e_sweethom.html - size 3K - 19 Mar 96

Endangered Species -- Minnesota -- Plants
Endangered Species -- Minnesota -- Plants. Leedy's roseroot (Sedum integrifolium ssp. leedyi) Minnesota trout lily (Erythronium propullans) Prairie...
http://straylight.tamu.edu/bene/esa/species/states/minnesota_plants.html - size 2K - 29 May 95

No Title
American Bittern Botaurus lentiginosus. Endangered Species List.
http://imlab3.landarch.uiuc.edu/~eskup/old_web/kvLA437-F95/proposals/wetland_habitat/bitt - size 193 bytes - 30 Oct 95

Endangered Species -- Minnesota -- Animals
Endangered Species -- Minnesota -- Animals. Butterfly, Karner blue (Lycaeides melissa samuelis) Eagle, bald (Haliaeetus leucocephalus) Falcon, American...
http://straylight.tamu.edu/bene/esa/species/states/minnesota_animals.html - size 2K - 29 May 95

Endangered Species
San Francisco Zoological Society. Endangered Species. This workshop provides information about the reasons species become endangered and why the loss of...
http://www.fwi.org/seaba/members/sfzs/sfzs-p2_1.html - size 3K - 27 Sep 95

ENDANGERED SPECIES ACT NEEDS REFORM
ENDANGERED SPECIES ACT NEEDS REFORM. by Congressman Richard Pombo. Thank you for the opportunity to present where we have come thus far in the endangered...
http://www.he.tdl.com/~rws/w/F-8/congress.htm - size 5K - 23 Aug 95

Endangered Species -- Michigan -- Plants
Endangered Species -- Michigan -- Plants. American hart's-tongue fern (Asplenium scolopendrium var. americana) Dwarf lake iris (Iris lacustris) Eastern...
http://straylight.tamu.edu/bene/esa/species/states/michigan_plants.html - size 2K - 29 May 95

Endangered Species -- Mississippi -- Animals
Endangered Species -- Mississippi -- Animals. Bat, Indiana (Myotis sodalis) Bear, Louisiana black (Ursus americanus luteolus) Clubshell, black (=Curtus'...
http://straylight.tamu.edu/bene/esa/species/states/mississippi_animals.html - size 3K - 29 May 95

Texas Organization for Endangered Species
Texas Organization for Endangered Species (T.O.E.S.) P.O. Box 12773, Austin, TX 78711 Contact Persons: Bob Murphy, Education Chairman; Clifton Ladd,...
http://nireinfo.srv.edu/unmaillib/Endanger/AOS/toes.html - size 3K - 10 Feb 95

Endangered Species -- Michigan -- Animals
Endangered Species -- Michigan -- Animals. Bat, Indiana (Myotis sodalis) Beetle, Hungerford's crawling water (Brychius hungerfordi) Butterfly, Karner blue...
http://straylight.tamu.edu/bene/esa/species/states/michigan_animals.html - size 2K - 29 May 95

p. **1** 2 3 4 5 6 7 8 9 10 11 12 13 14 15 16 17 18 19 20 [Next]

Jobs! · **About AltaVista** · **About Digital** · **Tips** · **Add URL** · **Feedback** · **Text-Only**

digital

FIGURE 3.3

useful to you. In such cases, you'll need to revise or expand your search. You have a number of options.

- Add more possibly related search terms with OR, to give your engine more choices.
- Change one or more of your terms by substituting synonyms (if *doctor* isn't working, try *physician*).
- Delete one or more terms from a multiple-term AND search to make it less restrictive.
- Switch one or more terms from a whole-word to a substring search to allow for plurals, past-tenses, and other forms of your keyword to be selected. Usually this is accomplished with a wildcard marker.
- Remove other restricting operations. (Removing double quotes, for example, allows a separate search on each keyword).

More likely, however, given the sheer quantity of sites and information on the Internet, a search query will turn up far too many hits to be useful, as in the sample search so far. In this case, you need to narrow and focus your search. In many cases, this will require you to narrow and focus your topic, common even when you're not using Internet resources. Even when you're doing library research, topics such as the *death penalty, abortion, the legalization of marijuana,* or *the Internet* have to be focused, either before or during research and drafting. Fortunately, when doing research using the Internet, this can be done explicitly and easily, with search engines.

An Internet search will immediately cause you to narrow your topic simply because more precise and limited keywords must be used. After this crucial step is completed, there are ways to refine the query itself:

- Add more keywords to an AND search.
- Remove one or more terms from an OR search.
- Exclude certain sets of hits (if you can detect a pattern that you can identify with a keyword) by using the boolean NOT or by removing wildcard markers from keywords.
- Add more restrictions to the search by including other operators to force whole-phrase searching (the adjacency operator) or using the proximity operator.
- Clarify the order of searching by grouping keywords more effectively with parentheses.

A Refined Search with AltaVista's Simple Query

Needless to say, 60,000 web pages roughly centered on the topic *endangered species* is far more than you need (or could possibly use). After exploring a few websites, thinking and reflecting, and focusing your thoughts, you refine your topic and decide to explore what is being done legislatively to protect endangered species—specifically the Endangered Species Act and whether it's adequate and effective. You also notice that plants are appearing frequently in your list of results; you hadn't anticipated that and want to exclude plants from your refined search to eliminate one source of unneeded information. Your refined query will read +*"endangered species act"* +*effective** -*plant**.

This query uses double quotes to force *endangered species act* to be treated as a unit in the search. The + forces AltaVista into a pure AND search, not allowing the fuzzy AND processes to affect the results by providing extraneous material. If a site doesn't contain the entire phrase *endangered species act,* in exactly that form (excepting the case of the letters), it won't show up in your final list. The + before *effective** forces the results to include only those pages that also contain some form of the word *effective,* e.g. *effective, effectively, effectiveness.* The -*plant** eliminates all pages which contain any form of the word *plant.* The results of the refined search are shown in Figure 3.4.

By refining your search, you have narrowed down your search to "about 1000" sites, and even though you still have access to only the most relevant 200, you are guaranteed a far more appropriate set of webpages to begin your research.

The following general principles apply to searching with any of the search engines available on the Internet:

- Find out what boolean and other logical operators the engine lets you use.
- Find out what the defaults are, particularly with regards to consecutive keywords.
- Construct your query and search with it.
- If necessary, refine your search.

EXERCISES

1. What is a search engine? How does it work?

2. What is the difference between browsing and searching?

3. What is a query? Give an example of one.

4. What are the major non-boolean logical operators used in constructing Internet search queries?

5. Compose a simple query for AltaVista that will find out, on the first page of its search results, where Karl Marx is buried.

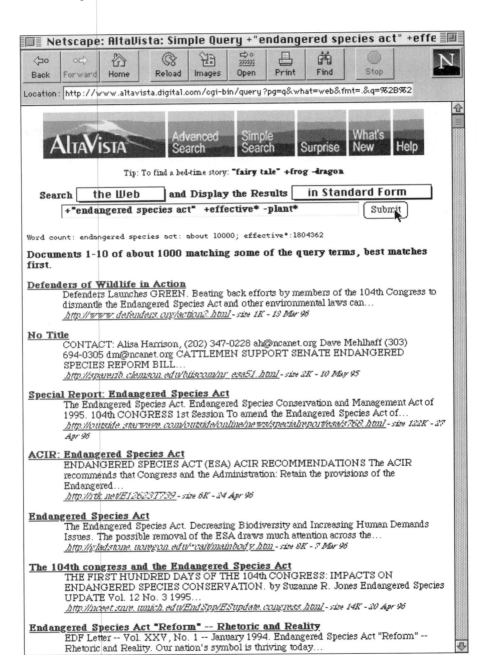

FIGURE 3.4

6. Try out the query in AltaVista. Are there any surprises? How can your query be refined?

7. Construct a simple query for AltaVista that will find information on Ulysses S. Grant's supposed drinking problem. While you're at it, construct a query that will find out his real name.

8. Browse the Yahoo directory http://www.yahoo.com/ . Find a general topic you think might be worth pursuing in a research paper; use Yahoo to narrow that topic, and find some initial sites where potentially useful information may be stored.

4

COMMUNICATING

One of the most popular uses of the Internet today is for communicating with other people. Since not all of the Internet's communication tools—IRC (Internet Relay Chat), in particular—are of obvious and immediate benefit to the researcher, in this chapter we will only deal with the three most useful Internet modes: email, Usenet newsgroups, and email discussion lists (or listservs).

These three modes are closest to regular, non-electronic modes. Therefore, you may feel more comfortable using them. Email is almost exactly like regular U.S. Postal Service mail, except that it's delivered almost instantaneously and it allows you to respond more quickly and easily. It's really quite simple

Email discussion lists are in some ways like magazines you subscribe to. When you subscribe to a magazine, every week or month the post office delivers a copy to you (and to everyone else who also subscribes). There are three major differences between discussion lists and magazine subscriptions: (1) the interval between deliveries is measured in hours or minutes rather than months or weeks; (2) it's not just one magazine—it's hundreds or more per month, each one having its own author; and (3) instantaneous, interactive responses are possible—if you read a message, or *post*, and want to respond to it in writing, you can, and everyone who subscribes to that discussion list receives your response as well.

Discussion lists are nearly always automated—run by robot server software that subscribes and unsubscribes users, receives and redistributes all postings to the list, and performs other functions such as searching the archives of the list when requested. The three most common software servers are Listserv, Listproc, and Majordomo. Strictly speaking, except in times of system failures or other problems, lists run themselves without human intervention.

Usenet, as mentioned in Chapter 1, is a collection of over 10,000 topically oriented electronic bulletin boards where lively discussions, arguments, and outright calumniations occur as people post, read, and reply to messages. The major difference between newsgroups and discussion lists is that you must actively seek out and read the messages on a newsgroup, while once you've subscribed to a listserv the messages arrive in your electronic mailbox automatically.

The value of these three modes varies widely—it's certainly possible to correspond electronically with authorities on particular subjects, if they have email accounts, just as you could through the regular mail. And for the researcher, immediacy is probably email's most useful benefit. The problem, of course, is finding the scholar's email address in the first place without any reliable white pages of email addresses. You will find much more congeniality and helpfulness through email than you will over the telephone or through regular mail. For some reason—perhaps because answering email is quicker and easier to do, and (unlike answering the phone) you can do it at your own convenience—people seem to respond more openly and reliably by email than by regular mail.

Listservs to a certain extent, and even moreso newsgroups, will tax your critical thinking abilities and your ability to separate nonsense and fallacious reasoning and lies from useful, accurate, and trustworthy information. Newsgroups and listservs are the epitome of democracy, since anyone with a computer and a modem can say anything to millions of people. Listservs tend to be slightly more professional and trustworthy, but this cannot be assumed. Newsgroups are free-for-all discussions.

FAQs

Most newsgroups and listservs have a regularly-updated list of answers to questions that are asked so often, they become a nuisance to readers. Someone compiles these frequently-asked questions (FAQs) and their answers and stores them somewhere (such as on a related website or gopherserver) for easy access. New subscribers to listservs are usually given this information when they subscribe, and newsgroup *newbies* (new readers unfamiliar with the particular newsgroup's subculture) are expected to seek out and read the FAQs for the group before they post questions. Not to do so is a breach of netiquette, and may often be met with the acronym RTFF, for *Read The [expletive deleted] FAQs.*

If you weren't advised of the location of a particular listserv's FAQs when you subscribed, you can usually find it using a good Web or

Gopher search engine. It's common (though not universal) practice to post a group's or a list's FAQs regularly—once a month or once every three months. Many Usenet groups post their FAQs regularly to the newsgroup *news.answers.* Try looking there first. In some instances, a list-serv or newsgroup may not yet have a FAQs list available.

Moderated versus Unmoderated

Another similarity of listservs and Usenet is the existence of moderators. By far, most lists and groups are unmoderated; that is, anything posted by anyone will show up. A moderator, however, is someone who reviews every posting and decides whether it's relevant, useful, tasteful, or whatever. If it meets the moderator's criteria (this is not as anti-free speech as it may seem), it is posted for all to read. If not, no one else sees it. The advantages are keeping discussions on topic, eliminating irrelevant or trivial posts (such as those whose entire message is "I agree"), and cutting down on messages containing gratuitous sex and violence.

EMAIL

Email is as useful a tool to the researcher as regular mail; in fact, because of the speed with which you can send and receive messages, it may be even more useful. You can correspond with friends, colleagues, classmates, your instructor, and noted authorities in the field. You can ask questions, get answers, work out problems, and even test out parts of drafts by emailing them to trusted readers. It may surprise you to know that many writers—probably even professors at your school—routinely correspond with each other in this way.

Finding Addresses

One of the ironies of the electronic age is that the best way to find someone's email address is to call or write and just ask. But sometimes that's not possible or convenient. Here are some Plan B's you can try when simply calling doesn't work for you.

First, guess. Email addresses (except those for CompuServe and some colleges) are often quite logical. The convention (though not the rule) is for an email address to consist of one's first initial and last name, with no space, followed by the @ sign (pronounced *at*), followed by the domain name (the institution's registered name) followed by a "." followed by the identifying suffix (usually, in academic cases, *edu*). If you know, for example, Jennifer Smith is at Ohio State University, try *jsmith@osu.edu* as her email address. Sometimes it works. To test it, either send her email, or *finger* her at that address. Finger is a small routine built into many computer systems that allows you to see some information about someone (e.g., if she's logged on or not, when she last logged on, and so on). If you finger someone and receive a response, that means you've got the right email address.

Second, try one of the search engines for the World Wide Web that allow searching for email addresses: Yahoo and Infoseek are the most prominent. (Actually, Yahoo uses the WhoWhere service, which you can access directly if you prefer; and Infoseek uses a similar service known as 411, which also may be accessed directly.) These sites maintain catalogs of email addresses, and may have the address of the person you want. A word of note: I tried five people whose email addresses I know, and neither WhoWhere nor 411 found any of them.

Third, there are a few older services, mostly registries, on the Internet that occasionally may be of some use. These are X.500 and Whois (pronounced *who is*). Both of these are available from Gopher menus or directly through telnet (see Chapter 6). They are cumbersome to use, however, and seem to be even less reliable in finding people.

When you see an address you think you might use someday—in a Usenet or listserv posting, for example—make an electronic note of it for later use. It's easy to keep a simple file of potentially useful addresses and let it grow to an enormous size, because it's so easy to search a word processing file or a database. Most mail reading programs like Eudora allow you to keep long lists of addresses in address books for easy reference.

And also remember, like everything else on the Net, email addresses may change frequently, for example, when a student changes schools or graduates, or when someone changes jobs or Internet Service Provider (ISP). An address that worked last month may not work this month.

DISCUSSION LISTS (LISTSERVS)

Even if the topics seem to be the same, listservs tend to be more academic and professional than do Usenet groups, as mentioned earlier. It's an odd phenomenon. This does not mean there will not be significant differences of opinion, however, nor that you can let down your critical evaluation guard.

Finding Discussion Lists

There is probably a listserv devoted to your special interest; you just have to find it. Fortunately, even though there are literally thousands of discussion lists, there is a resource for finding a particular one: it may be found on the World Wide Web at http://www.nova.edu/Inter-Links/listserv.html. A searchable directory limited to *scholarly* email discussion lists (which also includes a selection of Usenet newsgroups of interest to scholars) is maintained by Diane Kovacs and is available at http://n2h2.com/KOVACS/. If you don't have access to the Web, you can receive a full list of listservs via return email by sending a message to listserv@bitnic.educom.com. The subject line should be left blank, and the message should read *list global* and nothing more. A list of mailing lists is also available on the news.lists newsgroup, also available by anonymous ftp from rtfm.mit.edu (in the /pub/usenet-by-group/news.lists/directory).

Example

Go to Kovacs's page and perform a search for relevant listservs on the endangered species topic. Browsing would take too much time, as there are over 6,000 lists indexed here. Searching for *endangered* gives no results; searching for *species* gives one irrelevant result. We are searching too narrowly for this index. Try a broader term like *ecology*. Out of the first 40 lists shown, one—ENVIRONMENT-L—looks immediately promising. Click on ENVIRONMENT-L to get its full listing, which is as follows:

```
Directory:
   Ecology and Environmental Studies
Discussion Name:
   ENVIRONMENT-L
Topic:
   Maintained by the Center for the Environment at Cor-
nell University. It is available primarily for general
discussion of the Environment, particularly as it
relates to New York state, though wider discussion top-
ics are, of course, encouraged.


Subscription Address:
   listproc@cornell.edu
Moderated?
   No
Archives:
   Yes
Contact Address:
   Chris Stuart cs10@cornell.edu
Submission Address:
   ENVIRONMENT-L@cornell.edu
```

```
Keywords:
    Environmental Studies
VR:
    10th Revision 1/1/96
```

This tells you that the list server's address is listproc@cornell.edu—that's where you send the automated commands to subscribe, unsubscribe, etc. And the address of the list—where you send your postings so other subscribers can read them—is ENVIRONMENT-L@cornell.edu.

Participating in Listservs

Once you've found one or two listservs that look relevant to your subject, you should subscribe. The most important concept to remember is the difference between the server—the software that automates the workings of the list—and the list itself. You send commands—to subscribe, unsubscribe, or have your mail held—to the listserver (Listserv, Listproc, or Majordomo), not to the subscribers of the list itself. They can't subscribe or unsubscribe you, so don't send those messages to the list.

Let's say you want to subscribe to the list ENVIRONMENT-L. First, find the address of its list server from Inter-Links or the *Directory of Scholarly and Professional E-Conferences*. Again, make sure you have the list server's address, not the address of the list itself. In other words, if the address you're using doesn't begin with either "listserv," "listproc," or "majordomo," you have the wrong one.

To subscribe to ENVIRONMENT-L, in your email program type *listproc@cornell.edu* in the *To:* box. Leave the *Subject:* box empty (if you can—some email software refuses to allow you to send a message with no subject. In this case, type in anything; try *subscribe*. It should make no difference.) In the body of the message type the following words, *and nothing else:*

> *subscribe ENVIRONMENT-L@cornell.edu John Jones*

Obviously, type your own name instead of *John Jones*. Do not use your login name or other codes or abbreviations or nicknames—just your real first and last name. It's very important not to add anything else to the message—don't sign it, don't say "please," don't ask questions. Anything else confuses the listproc software. Remember, it's a robot software program—no human will be reading your request for subscription.

Soon, in a few minutes or an hour or two at the most, you will receive one or two messages by email: one simply confirms your sub-

scription and, in some cases, a longer one gives you additional instructions on how to use the listserv.

The acknowledgement for ENVIRONMENT-L is as follows:

```
Welcome!

You are now a subscriber to the ENVIRONMENT-L mail-
ing list.

Please save this message for future reference,
because it contains information you will need on manag-
ing your list subscription and for obtaining documenta-
tion and assistance.

Your subscription address
--------------------

Your subscription address for this list has been
recorded as:

    xxxxxxx@xxxx.xxxx.edu

To be recognized as a valid subscriber, you must
send all your postings and administrative commands from
that address.

Posting to the list
--------------------

To send mail to all other list subscribers, use this
address:

    ENVIRONMENT-L@cornell.edu

Be sure to use this address ***ONLY*** when you want
to send mail to EVERYONE ON THE LIST. Do not use this
address to issue administrative commands, described in
the next section.

Submitting administrative commands
--------------------
```

You have control over certain aspects of how you get mail from the list. This control is exercised via the submission of administrative commands directly to the "mailing list server", the machine/program that implements mailing lists at Cornell. The mailing list server is known as "listproc", and any administrative request must be sent to the server at this address:

    listproc@cornell.edu

Please note that mail sent to this address is processed by a machine, not a person. See the section on "Who to contact with problems" for information on how to reach a real person.

The section below on "Getting documentation" explains how to obtain a description of the various administrative commands that may be issued.

Your subscription password

Your password for this list is:

    XXXXXXXXX

This password applies only to this particular mailing list. You will need to use this password only when you need to change your subscription address, or if you wish to remove yourself from all lists maintained by the Cornell Mailing List server via a single command.

You may change this password, but note that mailing-list passwords are not secure. You should therefore not select the same password you use for logins, network identifiers, or other secure systems.

Getting documentation

For details on changing passwords and for a full description of all features and commands of this mailing-list system, send mail to:

listproc@cornell.edu

containing this single line of text:

HELP

A document tailored specifically for Cornell mailing lists is also available. It is called "How to Use Mailing Lists" (How To-61), and may be accessed via a World Wide Web page:

http://www.cit.cornell.edu/cit-pubs/mailing-lists.html

Who to contact with problems

If you encounter problems with this mailing list, please contact the owner(s):

cs10@cornell.edu

A second source of assistance is the Cornell mailing list manager, who oversees the running of the mailing list server. To reach the manager, send mail to:

listmgr@cornell.edu

In any correspondence about your subscription, please be sure to include:

-the name of the list in question

-a full description of what the problem is

-any error/notification messages you may have received.

How to unsubscribe from the list

To leave the list at any time, send mail to:

listproc@cornell.edu

containing this single line of text:

    UNSUBSCRIBE ENVIRONMENT-L

You must send this mail from the same email address you used to subscribe (namely, xxxxxxxx@xxxx.xxxx.edu).

****

The above material applies to all mailing lists maintained by Cornell. What follows is additional information provided by the owner(s) of the ENVIRONMENT-L list.

****

Welcome to environment-l!

This list is maintained by the Center for the Environment as a general discussion list on topics of the environment. We hope students, faculty, and staff at Cornell University as well as those outside the university will use it to discuss aspects of the environment as it relates to Cornell, the Ithaca area, and New York State, although wider area topics are encouraged as well.

The Center for the Environment will also use this mailing list to post announcements such as seminars, jobs, publications, and additions to our World Wide Web site. Subscription is open to anyone with an email account, so you are welcome and free to pass information on how to subscribe to this list to anyone. The Center for the Environment retains the right to unsubscribe anyone for gross misuse of the list.

Also, this list has been set up so that a reply to a message coming from environment-l will go out to the entire list, so be careful and check the to: field in your mail program to make sure you're sending it to the person/people you think you are. Thank you, and enjoy!

If you have any further questions you can reach me at:

```
--------------------
```

Chris Stuart
  cs10@cornell.edu
    Information Systems Manager Center for the
    Environment
    200 Rice Hall
    (607) 255-3972
    Department of Natural Resources
    204 Fernow Hall
    (607) 255-6578
    Cornell University, Ithaca, NY 14853
    http://www.cfe.cornell.edu—Center for
      the Environment Web
    http://www.dnr.cornell.edu—Cornell Dept. of
      Natural Resources Web

```
--------------------
```

If the list's FAQs are identified, find them and read them. Next, lurk. Simply read the messages as they pour into your mailbox daily, for a few weeks, until you've got the feel of the discussions and you have something to say or ask. You should not jump in immediately with a question or comment to a discussion list, just as you wouldn't walk up to a group of people and start talking before you knew what they were saying and doing.

Searching Listserv Archives

Many discussion lists keep archives of all their posts, so it's possible to check out a discussion that may have happened before you subscribed, or one that happened recently but that you didn't follow closely. An unexpected advantage of searching listserv archives rather than reading them as they occur is the filtering out of extraneous materials—often a list will have three or four or twenty-five topics (*threads*) under discussion simultaneously; the thread you want to follow is probably intertwined with dozens of other discussions. Wait until the discussion seems to have died out (rarely more than a week or so) and then retrieve only that thread. It makes it much easier to follow the discussion.

There are similar procedures for searching lists that use the Listserv and Majordomo software, which you usually receive in the first email from the list after subscribing. You search an archive by sending its *list server* (again not the list itself!) email instructing it to search for something, and, once it's finished its search, to email you the posts that meet your criteria. The rules for constructing your searches are strictly delineated, giving you specific terms to use.

USENET (NEWSGROUPS)

The overwhelming nature of the Internet is nowhere as apparent as in Usenet, over ten thousand (and counting) topically arranged free-for-all discussion groups. In all likelihood, there is a newsgroup (or a number of them) devoted to any topic you happen to be interested in.

Participating in Newsgroups

You don't actually subscribe to newsgroups in the same way as you do with listservs. Some news reading software (particularly the commercial online services such as America Online or CompuServe) seems to offer the option of subscribing, but in actuality what it does is seek out certain newsgroups that you specified and make a personal list for you, thereby simplifying the process. There is no formal subscription for newsgroups. Messages are posted (organized by topic), and you or your newsreader software must go out and retrieve them in order to read them and reply. There's no need to notify the newsgroup that you're a subscriber, and no need to unsubscribe or take any other formal steps.

Threads
Like email discussion lists, newsgroups follow certain discussion threads, subtopics that engender a running conversation for a few days or a few weeks at most. There may be many individual threads—postings and replies and new postings—occurring simultaneously. Many newsreader software packages will actually arrange the postings of a newsgroup into its threads to allow you to read one thread from beginning to end, without the distraction of trying to keep a number of threads in your mind at once.

A thread begins when one person posts a note—a question, comment, observation, occasionally a tangentially-related reply to a previous or current thread—to the group. Sometimes it generates little or no response. A question may be answered quickly and correctly (and often is) by another reader, and the thread goes no further. For example, someone may post a question with the subject "Ted Nelson's Real Name?" asking "Does anyone know what Ted Nelson's real first name is? I need it for some research I'm doing. Thanks in advance." The response, indicated with a subject of "Re: Ted Nelson's Real Name" and often appearing within minutes, will be "Theodor" and that's the end of the thread.

(Note: Though there are exceptions from time to time, Usenet postings generally are short, terse, and to the point. Netiquette advises against long, rambling posts.) Often, however, a post will spawn a week's worth of *Re:*'s, and you have a real thread to follow—the original seed post and the string of replies it initiated.

If, after reading the FAQs and lurking, you find a discussion you'd like to enter, use the Reply function in your newsreader (don't compose a new message, since doing so will start a new thread) and compose a brief, pointed, relevant reply. If you're replying to one particular person's post, name that person (most good newsreader software allows you to quote all or part of a post to which you're replying, and it will insert the author's name into your message as well). Sometimes, you may want to reply by email directly and privately to the author of a post, rather than broadcast your reply, either because you don't want to embarrass the author, or your reply is important to you but would be seen as trivial or off-topic by the rest of the list's readers. It's common to strike up useful email relationships with knowledgeable people in this way.

Searching Newsgroups

If you enter a group just as a particularly interesting discussion seems to be dying out, or want to see if a topic has been exhausted previously before you post a question or observation, search the archives.

Searching for newsgroup postings and threads is a bit trickier than searching listservs, however, because there is no standard way of archiving the materials. In fact, many newsgroups are not archived at all, so you may only be able to search the messages that remain on the news server.

If you have been able to find a FAQ list for the group, it should tell you if there are archives and where to find them—often on a Gopher server associated with the group. If so, you may simply access the appropriate directory on that Gopher server and either browse or search for interesting threads or posts. More likely, however, you will need to search. Your first stop will be DejaNews, a search engine on the WWW devoted exclusively to newsgroups.

A Sample DejaNews Search

Using your Web browser, go to the DejaNews homepage. If you have a graphical Web browser, you will be presented with the screen shown in Figure 4.1.

DejaNews allows a full set of boolean operators for constructing queries: AND (or the symbol &), OR (|), and AND NOT (&|). The default operator for a series of keywords is AND. Parentheses may be used to alter

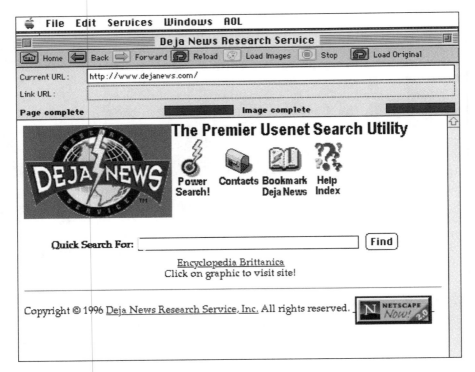

FIGURE 4.1

the order of operations within your query. In addition, wildcard searches (*), whole phrase adjacency searches (" . . . "), and proximity searches are allowed. A proximity search takes the form *word1 ^number word2,* which means that word1 must appear within the number of words specified for the posting to be found. For example, *Roadrunner ^25 Coyote* means to find only documents in which the keywords *Roadrunner* and *Coyote* appear within 25 words of each other.

DejaNews also allows you to limit your search to one particular author, subject heading, newsgroup, or creation date by using the operators ~a,~s,~n, or ~dc, respectively. Dates must be entered in the form YYYY/MM/DD (e.g., ~dc 1996/06/12, for a creation date of June 12, 1996). Parentheses and all other operators are permitted, with the exception of wildcards in dates.

To start, enter *"endangered species"* into DejaNews's query box. The double quotation marks force DejaNews to treat the words as a phrase and not as a simple AND query.

Other Searchers

A few of the WWW search engines—notably Infoseek and AltaVista—offer the ability to search newsgroups as well, simply by specifying Usenet rather than the World Wide Web as the range to be searched. See Chapter 5 for a full discussion of using those engines.

Critically Evaluating Usenet Postings

Usenet postings present the greatest challenge to your critical evaluation skills, because of the amount of "noise" you have to filter in order to get information. The vast majority of times, Usenet posters are just average people expressing their opinions—informed and misinformed, rational and biased, thoughtful and off-the-cuff. Occasionally, there will be a posting by an expert in a particular field who has substantial information to offer, but this is not that common. Ultimately, recognizing misleading, inaccurate, or useless postings is a matter of skill, experience, and taste. (Different people will place more or less trust in the posting of an enthusiastic Rush Limbaugh supporter, for example.) Here are some guidelines which may help as you gain experience in the Usenet world.

Consider your first impulse. Does the posting appear to contradict what you believe, what you've seen and heard firsthand, or what most other posters in the group are saying?

- Consider the motivation, biases, and outright prejudices of the poster.
- Recognize and critically examine the party line of both sides of an issue. If you agree with the poster, or most other authorities you've read appear to agree, put yourself in the position of someone who disagrees. How would that person react to this particular posting?
- Verify any information you get from Usenet with a second source. How much of what a poster writes is verifiable fact, how much is well-considered opinion, and how much is mindless ranting and raving?
- Take into account any inflammatory or blatantly prejudiced language. How does this influence credibility?
- Consider the poster and what you know about that individual, including membership in organizations, where employed, and so forth

An extended example of a Usenet thread and a critical analysis of it are included in Appendix 1. Read these to see how conversations, ideas, disagreements, corrections, and mistakes flow back and forth in a newsgroup. Following a discussion is fascinating, but the challenge is to keep your wits about you.

EXERCISES

1. Find an email discussion list (listserv) that you might be interested in. Lurk for a week or two. Can you find its FAQs? How would you characterize the tone of most of the postings? Are controversial issues tackled? Are there any flames? If so, for what reason? What seems to be a significant taboo on this list?

2. Do the same for a Usenet newsgroup. What differences do you see between the newsgroup and the email list?

3. If anyone seems particularly knowledgeable or authoritative on either the list or the newsgroup, send him or her a private email asking for clarification or further expansion of some point he or she made. Do you get an answer? If so, how would you describe the answer?

4. In a thread from either the newsgroup or the listserv, try to find an example of:

    a. flaming
    b. an unsupported assertion
    c. a misreading of someone's post
    d. an especially convincing argument
    e. an obviously biased poster

5. Find two different lists or newsgroups dealing with roughly the same topic. Contrast them: the tone, the willingness to either disagree or engage in verbal combat, the unwritten and unspoken assumptions behind the postings.

5

THE WORLD WIDE WEB

When you speak of the Internet today, most people think you're speaking of the World Wide Web. And in some ways that's true. The Web has so far outstripped the earlier Net technologies, that very little new development is taking place. With its intuitive interface, its interactivity, and its ability to present sound, color, and video, the Web has taken the Internet, the business world, and the other media by storm. One additional advantage for you is that most webbrowsers encompass all the earlier technologies: they can perform ftp and Gopher and WAIS. The intuitive interface available if you have a direct Internet connection (SLIP or PPP) allows you to just point and click, finding information and retrieving it, directly to your own computer.

The World Wide Web is generally thought to have been designed by Tim Berners-Lee at the Center for High-Energy Physics in Switzerland in 1991. Berners-Lee designed a prototype of a system that used hypertext links to allow users to move around (or browse) through large amounts of data, following patterns of associations built into the data by the people who assembled it, rather than looking up information in an index and trying to find it that way. The first user interfaces (clients) were text-based and selections were made with keypresses, but the growing popularity of graphical interfaces such as Macintosh and Windows made it inevitable that graphical software would be developed to utilize the structures Berners-Lee had developed. That software was a web browser known as Mosaic, and it revolutionized the World Wide Web, giving it the color, sound, interactivity, and hypertextuality that were latent in Berners-Lee's design. Though Mosaic has since been surpassed in popularity by Netscape Navigator, designed by one of the original programmers from the Mosaic project, Marc Andreessen, the concept of clicking a mouse and being transported to another place in the world is the defining characteristic of the World Wide Web.

THE STRUCTURE OF A WEBPAGE

When you click your mouse on a marked link on a webpage, here's what happens: first, your browser reads the URL contained in that link. This URL is invisible to you—it's hidden in the HTML code written by the author of the page. You computer then calls up the computer whose URL is listed. If a specific page is listed in the URL as well (that is, if the URL ends in the phrase *.html*), your computer will retrieve all the information from that page and your browser will read that information, decode it, and display the page on your screen. If the URL does *not* end in *.html,* your computer retrieves the information from the site's homepage and displays that homepage on your screen.

There are four potentially confusing terms you will hear concerning the World Wide Web: link, homepage, webpage, and website. A website is a collection of related pages stored together, analogous to a book or perhaps to a filing cabinet. It's common to speak of the "Apple Computer website" or the "Department of Education website," an organized and interlinked collection of webpages belonging to and pertaining to the general subject of the site. You can move around the site from page to page by clicking on specially marked places on the screen called links: often they are blue and underlined, if they are text; bordered by a blue square if they are images.

A webpage is a single screen of information, regardless of its length. (You may view different parts of it by scrolling up and down, but it's still one page of information.) The word *page* is actually a metaphor, because though a webpage resembles a page in a book in some ways (words and pictures), it can be any length and it can be accessed at any time. Pages do not need to be read in any particular sequence. Besides text, a page may contain animations, movies, sound, and, as you have already seen, interactive boxes called forms where you may enter information and cause something to happen.

A homepage is simply a special case of the webpage: the first page you come to when you arrive at a site. It normally is a master directory of all the pages stored on a site, perhaps with an identifying logo and an overview of what you will find on the other connected pages at the site. Usually there are links to more pages, both at the particular site and perhaps to other sites around the world that the author of the site has deemed related or interesting.

In addition to containing links to other pages at the site and around the world, a webpage typically contains a title and a number of headers. The title can be, and often is, invisible to you—it's written into the code that your browser reads, so your browser knows what the page's title is, but it may or may not be displayed. But a conscientious webmaster (the person who designs and/or maintains the site) will make sure the titles are meaningful and useful. A header is like a chapter title in a book or a Roman numeral heading in a formal outline: it indicates a unit of related information on the page. It appears in bigger, bolder type than the rest of the text on the page. Often the webmaster will place the title of the page in the first—or Level 1—header; sometimes the Level 1 header will simply refer to the first chunk of information on the page. Either way, titles and headers contain valuable and pointed descriptions of the content of a webpage or a website. You will see later that some search engines give you the option of searching only the titles or the first headers of webpages, markedly speeding up your searches and at the same time focusing your searches on prominent text rather than subordinate information.

A NOTE ON LYNX

Most of the discussion of search engines and the examples shown below will use various graphical webbrowsers such as Netscape, CyberDog, Mosaic, or the America Online browser. However, you have full access to the information on the Web even if you don't have access to a graphical interface. Nearly all computer systems on the Internet not offering a direct SLIP/PPP connection include a program called Lynx, developed at the University of Kansas for browsing the World Wide Web using a text-only interface. In the unlikely event that you don't have Lynx on your system, you may access a version of it via telnet at the following University of Kansas site: lynx.cc.ukans.edu.

Lynx allows you to navigate the Web without the use of a mouse. Instead of clicking a mouse, you select your choices with the up-arrow and down-arrow keys, and you activate your selection (the analogue of clicking the mouse) with the right-arrow key. Pressing the space bar allows you to scroll to the next screen of information on the webpage; pressing *p* (or -) takes you to the previous screen of information on the same webpage. If you press the left-arrow key, you are taken to the website you saw most recently. The = key gives you information on the website you are currently browsing, and the / key allows you to search for a particular word or phrase on the page. You may add a site's URL to your list of bookmarks with the *A* (not *a*) command.

One nice feature of Lynx is that it overcomes one of the most frustrating features of using a non-graphical dial-in account—the inability to download text and other files directly to your own desktop computer. Normally when you're using a text interface, your computer is nothing more than a dumb terminal passing instructions to your school's mainframe computer. When you ftp a file using a text interface, for example, you tell your school's computer to get a particular file, which then resides on your school's computer until you find a way to download it to your own computer. When Lynx downloads a file (which you initiate with the *D* command [not *d*]) it allows you to use a standard transfer routine such as Kermit, Xmodem, or Zmodem (one of which you must have on your own computer) to download directly to your own desktop PC. (This is the most notable feature missing from the telnet version of Lynx, by the way.)

But with Lynx, you have access to all the information available on the Web—you can't actually see all the graphics or hear all the sounds, but you can download them for later perusal with your own graphics viewer or sound player.

WEB SEARCH ENGINES

Like ftp and Gopher, the Web has its own set of search engines, but since it has become so popular, there is a much wider variety to choose from. Unlike Gopher and ftp, which have basically only one search engine each for finding information, the Web has, by some counts, hundreds, and no two are identical. Each has its own strengths and weaknesses; some offer more boolean operators than others, some index more webpages than others; some are faster. Perhaps the most important concept to remember when using a Web search engine is that no two will give exactly the same results when supplied with the same keywords. It's best, therefore, to try a number of different searches with different engines to ensure finding the most and best information.

To access the search engine, simply go to the website (i.e., enter its URL into your webbrowser's go to form) where it resides. In most cases, the first page you encounter at the site will be the query page: you will be presented with a form where you can type your keywords. Some sites initiate the search when you press the Enter key: some require you to click the mouse or otherwise select a button marked Search or Continue.

Some of the most useful and popular WWW search engines are AltaVista, Infoseek, Excite, Yahoo, Lycos, and WebCrawler. In addition, there are a number of websites that allow you to use more than one engine simultaneously: All4One and CUI are the best known currently.

All the engines treated below used spider technology; in addition, Yahoo, Excite, WebCrawler, and Infoseek offer directories for browsing.

ALTAVISTA

AltaVista (http://www.altavista.digital.com/) is a service operated by Digital Equipment Corporation. It is one of the most powerful, if not the most powerful, of the publicly accessible engines. It claims, as of this writing, to index 22 million webpages and over 11 billion words! In addition, it also can search Usenet newsgroups for articles. AltaVista offers two levels of search (simple and advanced) and a number of options within each level. It has extensive online help for both levels (some of which appears on the screen randomly as you log on; more complete help is available by clicking on the "help" button at the top of the screen), but tapping its full power requires an understanding of its complexity.

The Simple Query

When you first access AltaVista, you are presented with the page shown in Figure 5.1, which allows you to type one or more keywords and click on the Submit button. Your search is by default a simple search: at this level you have certain options for searching by keyword. The default search is the boolean OR: that is, if you tell AltaVista to search for *carbon monoxide* it will find all webpages containing either the word *carbon* or the word *monoxide*. In addition, if you enter your keywords all in lower case, the search will be case-insensitive; if, however, you enter some keywords with a mixture of upper and lower cases, you will force a case-sensitive search. So, if you want to find information on the British scientist James Watt, entering *watt* will bring up all the references to the scientist Watt as well as every other page that uses the word *watt*. To limit your search to the scientist, enter *Watt,* which will force a case-sensitive search and return only hits on the word with the uppercase *W.*

Other Options

You may force an AND search with the + symbol. Precede each keyword that you definitely want to appear in the found documents with a +. To find all the documents which contain both *James* and *Watt,* construct the search phrase *+James +Watt.* To exclude a specific keyword, use the - symbol: *+Queen +Elizabeth +II -ship* will eliminate all hits on documents containing the word *ship,* which will help limit your findings to the monarch and not the vessel. An even simpler way to conduct this search would be to use the adjacency operator, which in AltaVista's simple

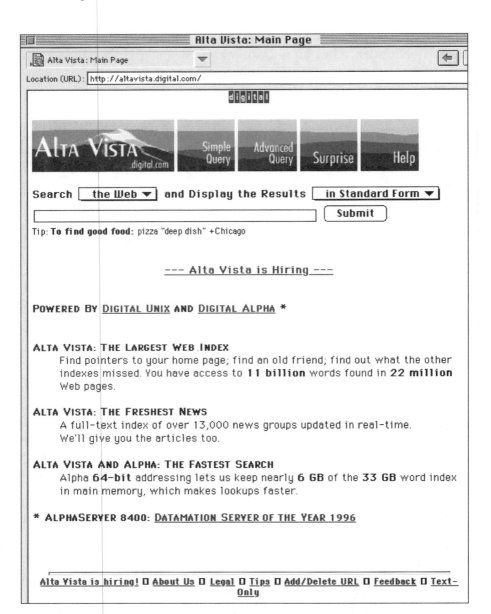

FIGURE 5.1

search is the enclosing double quote marks: " ". Enclosing *"Queen Eliza-beth II"* in double quotes causes AltaVista to treat the whole phrase as a unit and search for that entire unit, rejecting hits on simply *Queen* or *II* or *Queen Elizabeth* or *Elizabeth II*. Likewise, *"james watt"* (with or without capital letters) restricts hits to only documents which contain that whole phrase, unbroken.

Wildcard (substring) searches are also possible using the * symbol. Entering *Mexic** will return hits on documents containing *Mexico, Mexican, Mexicans,* and *Mexicali,* among others. It's useful for broadening searches to include plurals and other forms of base words, but, as always, may very easily produce tens of thousands of hits, usually more than you want. The * operator can only be used at the end of a string of letters, may only follow base words of at least three letters, and will only match up to a maximum of five lower-case letters.

You can force AltaVista to look only at URL links or From addresses in Usenet postings or webpage titles by entering the appropriate phrase followed by a colon. Thus, entering *subject:Bosnia* will search Usenet "subject" fields only and return only those with *Bosnia* in the subject field, ignoring any possible occurrences of *Bosnia* in the text of the postings. Phrases used to restrict websearches are *anchor:, applet:, host:, image:, link:, text:, title:,* and *url:.* Usenet terms are *url:* (to indicate email addresses in the From: field), *subject:, newsgroups:, summary:,* and *keywords:.*

One final note: the hits you get from an AltaVista simple search are ranked according to a few rudimentary principles: how near the beginning of the document your keywords appear, how near each other your keywords appear in the document, and how frequently your keywords appear in the document. A document with all your keywords at the beginning, with your keywords grouped closely, and with many occurrences of your keywords will appear high on the list of hits.

The Advanced Query

AltaVista's advanced query offers all the options of the simple query for refining your searches (though you generally indicate them differently), plus many more. All the boolean operators are available, but must now be used explicitly: you must use AND, OR, AND NOT, and NEAR or their respective counterparts &, |, !, and ~. The NEAR (or proximity) operator finds documents in which the two keywords are within ten words of each other—useful for names and titles, for example *King NEAR Henry NEAR England** will find references to *Henry IV, King of England* and *England's King Henry VIII.* Double quote marks are still the adjacency phrase indicator. Terms for restricting searches in both websearches and Usenet searches are the same as in simple queries, as well.

The order in which AltaVista looks at your keywords may be altered with parentheses: *(apple AND pie) OR ("ice cream")* will return a different set of hits than will *apple AND (pie OR "ice cream")*. The first will find all documents that contain both *apple* and *pie* and then find another set that contains the phrase *ice cream*. It will then return a list of both sets. The second search phrase will first find a set that contains either *pie* or *ice cream* and then, from that set, return only those that also contain the word *apple*. (Capitalization rules in the advanced query work the same as they do in the simple query—all lower case means a case-insensitive search; any upper case triggers a case-sensitive search.)

In addition, the ranking of the hits in an advanced query offers more control: if one particular item or term is more important than another in your search phrase, you may choose to assign it greater weight in the Ranking Field box, and AltaVista will then place documents meeting those specified criteria higher on the list of hits.

Conclusions

AltaVista is one of the most powerful search engines for the World Wide Web and Usenet today. It allows you to construct complex search phrases that let you pinpoint the information you seek without a lot of trial and error, so you get all the information you need and only the information you need. Despite the awe-inspiring amount of information it indexes for searching, it is surprisingly fast. But, with all this power comes the need for you to master the procedures of full boolean searches and the idiosyncratic set of symbols used to describe those searches.

INFOSEEK

Infoseek (http://www.infoseek.com/) is another of the very powerful and precise WWW search engines. It allows you to construct accurate searches, and it does so without requiring much knowledge of boolean operators on your part. Its initial first-level search is simple to master, asking you simply to "type a few words that describe what you want to find," consciously avoiding any hint of the arcane boolean language. In fact, its only real drawback is the size of its database; compared to AltaVista, for example, it indexes relatively few websites.

Constructing Queries with Infoseek

When you first enter the Infoseek site, you will be greeted by the page shown in Figure 5.2. Note that you have the option of searching either the World Wide Web (which is what you will do most of the time), Usenet newsgroups, or email addresses.

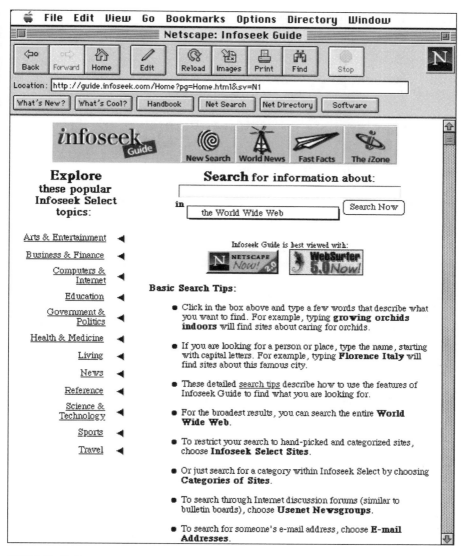

FIGURE 5.2

In constructing your queries, Infoseek allows something resembling natural language searches, which means that you don't necessarily have to use boolean operators in your queries. You simply enter some keywords, which can be phrases that sound like normal English, into the query box and Infoseek searches for them. Actually, all this means is that Infoseek's default search is what's called a *fuzzy AND* search, meaning that Infoseek will first find the phrase you type, as if it were doing an AND search, and then continue to find sites with one or two of your keywords, as if it were doing an OR search, while ignoring small, common words entirely. Thus, entering the natural language phrase *the care and feeding of Irish Setters* is equivalent first to the boolean phrase *care AND feeding AND Irish and Setters,* and when Infoseek exhausts those sites, it switches to the phrase *care OR feeding OR Irish OR Setters.*

If *fuzzy AND* natural language searches are not adequate for your task, however, with Infoseek you have a number of true boolean options for constructing your query. You may force an AND search with a plus sign, and you can exclude certain keywords with the minus sign (a boolean NOT). There is no formal OR operator. Capitalizing a word forces a case-sensitive search; capitalizing successive words (as in names) forces Infoseek to perform a case-sensitive search on the entire string as a unit (e.g. *Abraham Lincoln* finds only sites with that entire phrase intact; it will not find sites that contain both *Abraham* and *Lincoln* separately.) Commas may be used to separate series of names: *Abraham Lincoln Andrew Johnson* would yield no results; *Abraham Lincoln, Andrew Johnson* would yield sites containing the names of both Presidents. Enclosing phrases in double quotation marks and joining words with a hyphen have the same effect: entering *"beef stew"* or *beef-stew* limits hits to sites containing only that specific phrase.

Infoseek also provides a proximity operator: enclosing keywords in square brackets will find sites in which the keywords appear within one hundred words of each other. There are no provisions for a wildcard search, and there is no way to group keywords with parentheses.

To search, choose whether you want to search the Web, newsgroups, or the email database, then enter your keywords in either natural English or a carefully constructed boolean phrase into the Search for: box and click on the "seek now" button.

Infoseek also ranks its findings, using a complex mathematical system to determine what it thinks is the relevance of a particular site to your initial request, using a 1 to 100 scale, 100 being the most relevant site. If your keywords appear a number of times on a site or if your keywords are phrases or relatively uncommon words, sites found will be ranked higher. When Infoseek completes its search and presents you with its findings, it will provide you with the clickable URL of each site, a brief description of the site, and an option to find similar sites. Clicking on this item has the effect of telling Infoseek that a particular site looks promising, and it should find more like it, ignoring other potentially less useful sites.

Browsing in Infoseek

In addition to its spider-based index, Infoseek also maintains a directory of popular sites, arranged in hierarchical categories. Currently its categories are Arts and Entertainment, Business and Finance, Computers and Internet, Education, Government and Politics, Health and Medicine, Living, News, Reference, Science and Technology, Sports, and Travel. Clicking on any one of these items takes you to another menu.

Providing directories in conjunction with the primary search engine capabilities is becoming more popular; the primary value of such a provision is allowing you to limit your search initially to a primary category, speeding up the search slightly and eliminating a large number of extraneous hits.

Browsing the directories of Infoseek or any of the directories supplied by the major search engines is useful when you're not sure of a topic, not sure what information may be available on a general topic you may be considering, or not sure what the major issues and sources of information may be.

YAHOO

Yahoo was the first of the very popular search engines, even though in its original incarnation it was more a directory than a search engine. In fact, its real strength to this day is its directory; its search engine is less powerful than others.

Constructing Queries with Yahoo

Yahoo offers an easy to use interface for its search engine, but it does not offer a full range of boolean operators for constructing queries. The initial Yahoo search screen appears in Figure 5.3.

Notice first its full directory listing, with a sampling of useful subdirectories listed as well. The actual search engine and its query box are decidedly less prominent than in other engines. Click on the "options" indicator to get a screen with pop-up menus for selecting the available query operators.

Yahoo offers essentially three choices:

- boolean OR or boolean AND
- substring or Complete Word
- number of hits (Yahoo calls them *matches*) to display

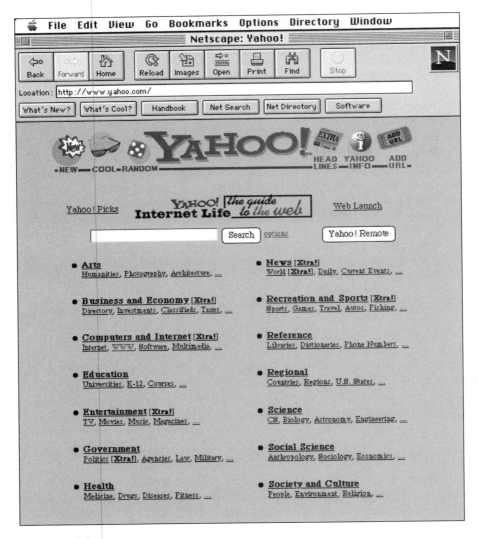

FIGURE 5.3

The search interface revealed by "options" is clean and uncluttered, making it ideal for quick searches that you anticipate will yield appropriate results with a minimum of tinkering with your query. Choices are made with pull-down menus rather than typing in operators and conditions, so that constructing actual query phrases is both unnecessary and impossible. If you can describe the set of information you're looking for with a simple query, Yahoo is a functional search engine. If you need to construct more complex queries, Yahoo is not so useful.

Browsing with Yahoo

Yahoo's strength is the depth of browsing it offers. It collects its websites into fourteen hierarchical categories:

- Arts
- Business and Economy
- Computers and Internet
- Education
- Entertainment
- Government
- Health
- News
- Recreation and Sports
- Reference
- Regional
- Science
- Social Science
- Society and Culture

With a number of subcategories displayed underneath the major categories, it's possible, if you recognize a major subject field you'd like to browse, to go directly to that page. You can refine your browsing through a number of levels underneath any categories before you actually come to a page of useful sites rather than lists of subcategories or sub-subcategories.

Following the Government branch, for example, brings you to the second level in Yahoo, a list of subcategories:

- Agencies
- Citizenship
- Conventions and Conferences
- Countries
- Documents
- Embassies and Consulates
- Executive Branch
- Federal
- Employees
- Institutes
- Intelligence
- International Organizations

- Judicial Branch
- Law
- Legislative Branch
- Military
- News
- Politics
- Reengineering
- Research Labs
- Student Government
- Technology Policy
- U.S. Budget
- U.S. States

The numbers following each subcategory tell how many sub-subcategories each contains. In addition, you have the option of clicking on *Sub Category Listing* for a complete hierarchical listing of all subcategories and their branches at once—useful if you know where you're going immediately and don't want to step down through level after level to get to a particular listing. Clicking on *indices* isolates for you a list of just the different indices contained in the various levels under each category. For example, clicking on *indices* at the Government level brings up the page (shown in Figure 5.4) of links to useful governmental indices.

Each of the listings on this page takes you to a Governmental WWW-based index of useful subject matter, from which you may link to any of the listings, such as *Government Resources on the Web*.

Yahoo also combines the search and browse functions. At any level of the browsing hierarchy, it's possible to construct a search query and search within that level (or search all of Yahoo), so that it's possible to narrow a search first by browsing, limiting your possible sites to just those Yahoo has listed for a particular subcategory. This useful feature is an alternative method of narrowing your search and focusing your efforts.

LYCOS

Lycos is a search engine operated by Carnegie-Mellon University. Its strength is in the number of sites and words it claims to index. It probably rivals AltaVista in the sheer amount of information it contains in its index. Other features include an array of simple pop-up menus for controlling a number of features, such as the tightness of fit of the results Lycos returns, making it possible to vary the amount of information you

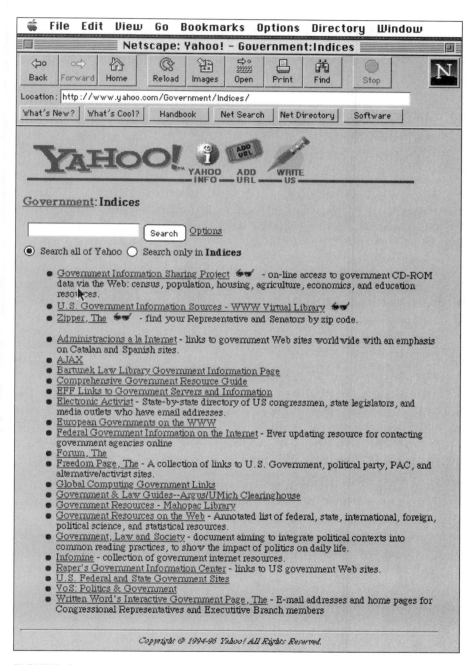

FIGURE 5.4

find depending upon how precisely you know what you're looking for. A looser search allows for more exploration and more chance of a serendipitous find; a tighter search more nearly guarantees you'll find only what you're looking for and little or nothing else.

Searching with Lycos

Lycos offers a small set of boolean and other logical operators for constructing queries. It uses the + to force an AND search, a - to indicate a boolean NOT, a . (period) to indicate a whole-word search, and a $ as the wildcard character to indicate string searches. The default search is a boolean OR. Lycos also uses a complex algorithm to rank its list items according to their computed relevance. At the time of this writing, Lycos has just added a separate directory service—known as A2Z—to its repertoire, but Lycos itself has no directory.

In addition to looseness/tightness of fit, Lycos also allows you to approximate the workings of parentheses with a pop-up menu of Match x Terms. You may specify how many keywords Lycos is to group into parenthetical AND sets as it searches. A query of *civil war generals* with Match 2 Terms selected would be treated by Lycos as two separate searches: *(civil AND war) OR generals* and *civil OR (war AND generals)*. Both sets would be returned as hits, ranked according to Lycos's algorithms.

Lycos's main search screen (accessed after selecting Expanded Search from the opening screen) appears in Figure 5.5.

Using the operators available, you may enter your query into the box. With the pop-up menus, you may change the default search type from OR to AND or you may choose to match from 2 to 7 of your keywords at a time. The Loose match default may be changed in five increments from loose to tight match, and Lycos may be reset to display 20, 30, or 40 matches at a time instead of the default 10.

The fourth pop-up menu displayed, "standard results," allows you to control how much detail Lycos returns in its listings. The default standard results displays a list of the titles and rankings of the found set; standard and detailed display more detail: an abstract of the content of the pages and a verbatim reproduction of the opening lines of the found pages, respectively.

WEBCRAWLER

WebCrawler is a search engine now operated by GNN (a subsidiary of America Online). In its original incarnation, WebCrawler was a very clean and simple search engine, indexing fewer sites than some of the

FIGURE 5.5

other giants like AltaVista or Lycos, offering few frills for constructing queries, and containing no directory. Its most recent update has seen it begin to try to compete with the giants, offering boolean searches, a larger index, and a directory. Its interface is still clean and simple, providing a query box and handy hints-of-the-day for constructing queries.

Searching with WebCrawler

On its main search page (Figure 5.6), WebCrawler offers, in addition to the query box, two pop-up menus: one to switch between displaying *titles* (the default) or *summaries,* and one to select the number of entries to list: 10, 25 (the default), or 100.

WebCrawler allows for queries using the standard boolean operators AND, OR, and NOT. The default search is a boolean OR. In addition it offers a configurable proximity operator, NEAR/x, where x is the span of proximity of words you desire, for example, NEAR/25. Either double quotes (" . . . ") or the ADJ operator indicates phrases, and parentheses may be used to change the order of operations.

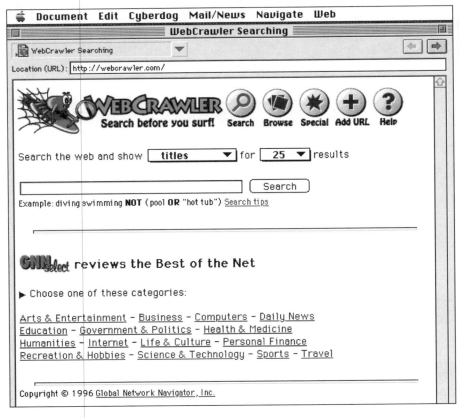

FIGURE 5.6

OPEN TEXT

Open Text is probably the easiest to use of the major Web search engines. In its Power Search mode, it allows you to assemble your queries, almost in a paint-by-number manner, rather than having to construct a query by remembering which operators a particular engine allows and how they are represented. Open Text's search interface (Figure 5.7) provides three query boxes, and a number of pop-up menus to indicate the relationship between the three keywords or simple phrases entered and to indicate where Open Text should search.

A Sample Search with Open Text

Open Text's Power Search mode begins by presenting three query boxes, three pull-down range indicators for choosing where to search

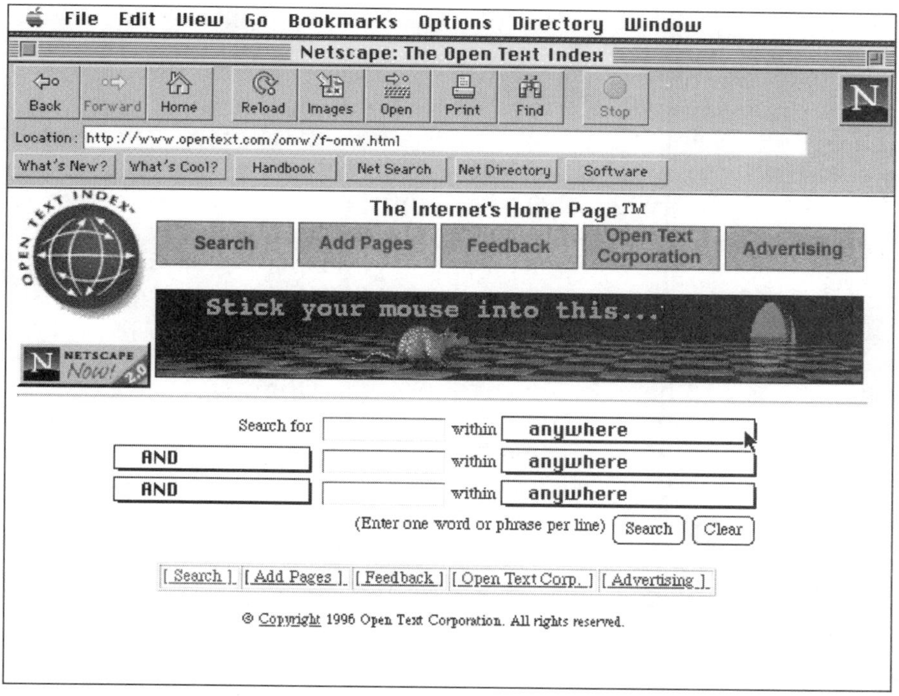

FIGURE 5.7

("within"), and two pull-down menus for choosing the boolean or logical connection between query items.

The query boxes may contain a single word or phrase; the search conducted on the contents of the query is case-insensitive. Other than that, it is a whole-word, exact match search. In other words, searching on *book* will find *Book* and *book* but not *books;* searching on *Old Testament* will find *old testament* but not *Mary Gold's last will and testament.* If you need a substring or wildcard search, you must approximate it with the boolean OR, for example, *book* and *books* in successive query boxes joined by OR.

The options for range are "anywhere" (the default), "summary," "title," "first heading," and "URL." Selecting "anywhere" performs a full-text search of all websites in Open Text's index; selecting "title," "first heading," or "URL" limits Open Text's search to just those particular components of the webpages in the index (see The Structure of a Webpage, at the beginning of this chapter). The "summary" is Open Text index's overview of the contents of the webpage, made up of the title of the page, its first heading, and other significant text found on the page. The summary is unique to Open Text and resides in Open Text's index— it is not an actual part of the webpage itself. Specifying one of these other ranges is a valuable way of limiting your search right from the beginning. If you find (or suspect that you will find) too much information with a full-text search, limit your search to just titles of webpages. Titles in well-designed webpages are usually precise and descriptive, so limiting your search to titles will eliminate the tangential or even unrelated pages that just happen to mention your keyword in passing.

The logicals available for joining keywords are boolean AND, OR, and BUT NOT, as well as NEAR and FOLLOWED BY. The logicals AND, OR, and BUT NOT work exactly as you'd expect boolean operators to work. The NEAR and FOLLOWED BY operators find pages in which the keywords joined by either of these two are within 80 characters (not words!) of each other (NEAR) or in which the second keyword follows within 80 characters of the first (FOLLOWED BY).

The absence of parentheses makes constructing very complex queries difficult. The query is read in a ruthlessly linear left-to-right (or in this case, top-to-bottom) fashion—the first keyword, the operator, the second keyword, the operator, etc. Open Text, in essence, searches its index for all occurrences of the first keyword, and then, using that found array of pages, applies the second keyword with its operator to that, and so on, constructing a new found set with each operation. If you want to, for example, find pages for automobiles but exclude Porsches and Ferraris [i.e., the boolean construction *automobiles NOT (Porsche or Ferrari)*], you would have to use *automobiles BUT NOT Porsche BUT NOT Ferrari.* This would find all pages containing the whole word *automobile,* then first eliminate from that set of pages all those containing *Porsche,* and then in another pass eliminate all those remaining that contain the word *Ferrari.* If you wanted to allow for both singulars and plurals, you would have to use the construction *automobile OR automobiles BUT NOT Porsche BUT NOT Porsches BUT NOT Ferrari BUT NOT Ferraris.* It's possible, in some instance, that you'll *never* be able to construct the exact query you need. But it's also rare that you'll ever need to construct such highly specialized queries.

Let's take an in-depth look at an actual search using Open Text. We'll begin by searching webpages for the whole phrase *endangered species* (Figure 5.8). Clicking on the "Search" button brings the results shown in Figure 5.9.

Even limiting your search to titles has found 3,195 sites that may contain information you need. You could browse all 3,195 sites, or (since Open Text also ranks its hits) you could just browse the first few or first few hundred, if you had the time. But you probably don't. You need to refine your query in order to get the number down to something

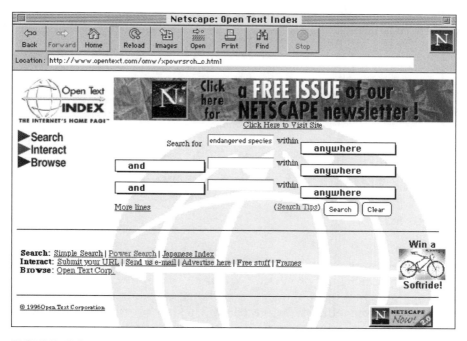

FIGURE 5.8

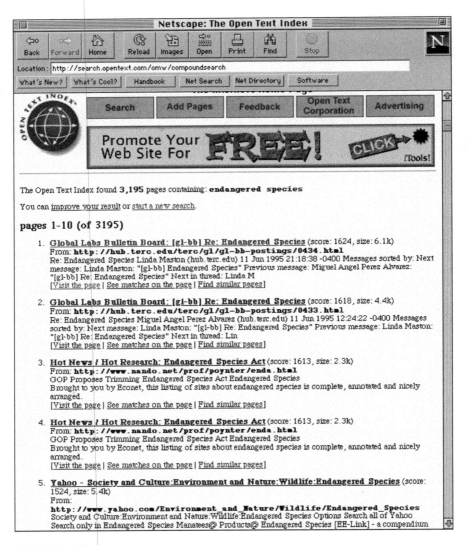

FIGURE 5.9

manageable. Suppose you're interested in effectiveness of the legislation and other policies in protecting endangered species; you notice this search has turned up references to endangered plant species as well as animals. So you refine your search by clicking on the "improve your results" link and constructing the query *endangered species (anywhere) AND effective (anywhere) BUT NOT plants (anywhere).*

Figure 5.10 shows the results of this narrowed search—238 hits. Better, and probably workable with careful browsing of highly ranked sites. But, let's narrow it further, to concentrate on documents whose major focus is endangered species, not those that mention them briefly. Such

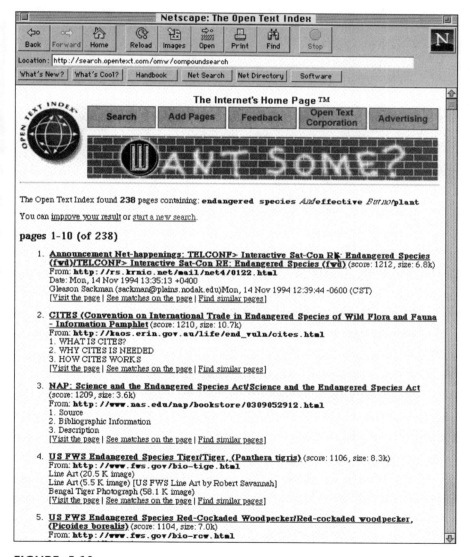

FIGURE 5.10

pages, if they're well-created, will mention *endangered species* in their titles. Let's perform the same search but limit the search to pages which contain the exact phrase *endangered species* in their titles by choosing "titles" from the pull-down "within" menu. Figure 5.11 shows the results of this narrowed search.

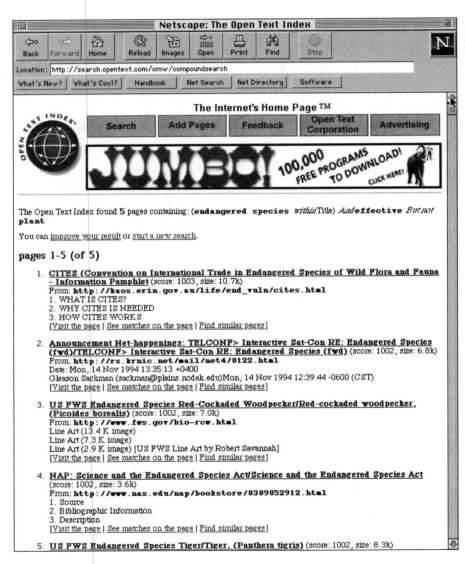

FIGURE 5.11

Now you have five sites to begin examining, each of which you know is precisely focused on the evolving sense of your topic.

A FINAL NOTE ON SEARCHING THE WWW

No two search engines will turn up exactly the same set of websites when given exactly the same query. Therefore, it's important to use a variety of engines and approaches to be sure you've covered your topic adequately. You should begin cultivating a sense of which engines you especially like, but be aware that different engines work better than others in certain circumstances. Make mental notes (or written ones, if you need to) of the strengths and weakness of each. See Table 5.1 for examples.

TABLE 5.1   **Search Engines**

Engine	Strengths	Weaknesses
AltaVista	**Powerful;** most complete coverage of the Web; complete set of boolean and logical operators for queries; two levels of search; can search Usenet and Web.	No directory for browsing
Infoseek	Two levels of search; full boolean and logical set; directory for browsing; **can search Web, Usenet, and email addresses.**	Relatively small index
Lycos	**Size of index** rivals AltaVista's; can adjust tightness of fit of search; some pop-up menus to allow for query construction.	More difficult than necessary; limited set of booleans and logicals
Open Text	Two levels of search: Power Search allows for **menu-based construction of queries;** can specify range to be searched.	Relatively small index
WebCrawler	**Quick;** boolean operators accessible by pop-up menus.	Limited set of logicals; can only search titles or summaries
Yahoo	**Best directory** for browsing; can search within levels of directories; pull-down menus for query construction.	Limited logicals for searching

In general, all the Web search engines are powerful and extremely fast. In fact, speed is generally not an issue, as the length of time to search is almost identical among all the search engines. Generally, power is good, but sometimes the power of AltaVista or Infoseek can overwhelm, and a quick and dirty search with WebCrawler can be more effective because it's more pointed. Finally, there will be times when constructing an elaborate query is more trouble than it's worth. Construct a good if approximate query, and browse and refine. It's often quicker.

EXERCISES

1. What is the difference between a search engine and a directory?

2. Explain how a spider works. How does this affect what materials are in an engine's database?

3. What are the parts of a URL? Give an example of a URL and explain what each part means.

4. What is a query?

5. Explain in your own words how boolean operators and other logical operators work in a query. Give an example of a complex query, using both boolean and other logicals, and explain how it will be parsed. What kinds of information do you expect it to find?

6. Use your query in your favorite search engine. Are there any surprises?

7. Enter a simple search with minimal boolean operators into WebCrawler. How many documents does it find? Enter the same search into AltaVista. How many documents does it find? How do the two searches contrast?

8. Make a personal chart for yourself of the strengths and weaknesses of each of the major search engines. Keep adding to it as you gain more experience with websearching.

6

OTHER INTERNET TECHNOLOGIES

In the early days of the Internet (pre-1990, actually), using the Internet meant being one of a small group of programmers who were comfortable typing strange, memorized commands from an impossible-to-use operating system known as Unix. If you wanted to copy a file, for example, you typed *cp*—not too hard to remember. To delete a file, you typed *rm*—and it gets worse. Finding information basically required asking one of the select Few for its name and location. Transferring a file from someone else's computer to your own meant using a set of conventions called *file transfer protocol,* or *ftp* for short.

Sometimes, on one of those few computers elsewhere in the world, there resided a program or some data that you wanted to use as your own. A routine called *telnet* was written to allow your computer to act as a terminal hooked to the distant computer so you could issue commands from thousands of miles away.

In 1991, programmers at the University of Minnesota decided there must be an easier way to perform all these functions. They designed a simple, menu-driven interface that allowed the user to choose from a list of options without remembering all the obscure commands needed to telnet and ftp to and from other computers. They called this system Gopher, after the school athletic teams' mascot; in some ways it became the second revolution of the Internet. Gopher performed ftp and telnet operations automatically, silently, invisibly. Suddenly, the Internet became easy to use—you didn't have to know a single secret command. People who never before had attempted to use information stored on all those networked computers worldwide began "tunneling through gopherspace." Simultaneously, gopherspace began growing as more and more organizations and institutions made information accessible on their Gopher servers.

Around the same time, another approach to simplifying the locating and accessing of stored information was being developed by a consortium of information users led by, among others, Apple Computers Inc. and Dow Jones. One of the problems Internet users encountered was that nearly every database of information stored on every computer used a different file format; every database looked different, with a different set of commands and routines to learn and remember. This problem was solved by a tool known as WAIS, short for Wide Area Information Server. WAIS allows you to actually search—using standard keyword and boolean techniques—for a database containing information that you may want, and it returns to you a standardized list of potentially useful databases from which you may then choose. A second search of those chosen databases then returns to you actual documents and information.

Many of the functions and advantages of WAIS were eventually subsumed into Gopher, so that simply by knowing how to use Gopher—not a daunting task—you were able to use telnet, ftp, and WAIS as well.

As you saw in Chapter 5, the latest revolution in the Internet—the World Wide Web and its graphical browsers—has subsumed even Gopher, and these early technologies are even less crucial to the researcher today than they were three short years ago.

Why, then, you may ask, do I need to know them at all? If WWW browsers such as Netscape do all this for me, why do I need to know anything at all about ftp or WAIS? The answer is, in a word, completeness. There is information available by ftp or WAIS which is not available over the Web and is not indexed by any of the Web search engines. The search engines used by the Web are far more comprehensive than those used by any of the tools covered in this chapter, but they are not 100 percent complete. No single search engine has complete coverage of everything on the Internet. The Internet is like a library that has converted to a computerized index of its holdings, but still maintains some records of old materials in its card catalog. If you want to find everything useful in that library, you have to know how to use both tools.

Second, not everyone has access to the newest and slickest graphical Web technology. Many students have only text-based access to the Internet, and still need to know how to manipulate the earlier tools in order to find and retrieve appropriate information.

TELNET

Telnet by itself is technically not a search-and-retrieve tool. What it does is allow "remote login": you can hook your computer to a distant computer or network over telephone lines, and actually operate that distant computer through your own computer. You can sit at your desktop computer in California and search the catalog of the Harvard library just as if you were in Cambridge.

A sample of remote computers which allow remote login via telnet includes NASA's Spacelink, a repository of NASA information made available to the public; the Weather Underground, an on-line University of Michigan source of up-to-date weather information, ski reports, hurricane information, and so on; any number of libraries around the world; and a variety of local campus- and community-based bulletin board systems (BBS).

With telnet, however, you still need to know all the commands of the remote computer, and you need to be granted access to that computer in the first place. But if these conditions are met, you instantly have access to computers and files and software from anywhere in the world. It's important to remember that telnet by itself gives you no new technologies or tools beyond those that reside on the remote computer into which you've logged. It just lets you use somebody else's computer for a while.

Using Telnet

Let's look at a typical use of telnet: logging into a remote library's catalog and searching through it. Remember exactly what you're doing here, however. With telnet, you won't be able to read the books or check out anything on-line—you're just looking through the catalog of the library's holdings. But there is still some limited value for the researcher in this capability. You can speed up interlibrary loan services when you request a book through your own library if you know that a particular library has the book you want. You can check the spelling of an author's name, an exact title, a copyright date, or a publisher for those late night final-draft sessions when you're putting together your research paper's Works Cited page and have neglected to get a vital piece of information.

Most Internet accounts, even non-graphical dial-in accounts, offer the telnet function. Usually, it's accessed at the prompt by typing in the command *telnet.* Graphical interface users will use a program called NCSA Telnet, free software from the National Center for Supercomputing Applications that has become the standard for both Windows and Macintosh Internet users.

The library of Dartmouth College has its catalog and a number of other resources available online, although some of the resources are restricted to Dartmouth users. To get to the Dartmouth library's on-line resources, telnet to lib.dartmouth.edu, where you will be greeted by the screen shown in Figure 6.1.

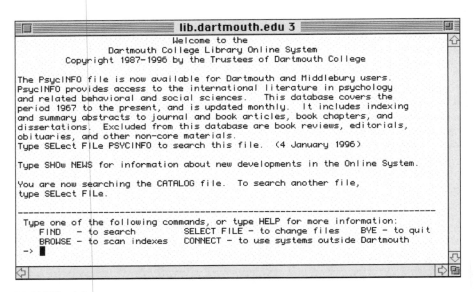

FIGURE 6.1

You are now using the Dartmouth library's computer system, via tel-net, just as if you were on the Dartmouth campus. Now let's get down to business. Say you've heard of a book about the downside of the elec-tronic revolution (how books and reading skills may disappear in the future), and the author's name is Birkerts, but you know very little else about the book. Where do you start? A Help command tells you that the Dartmouth on-line library expects its searches to be in the form *find <type> <keyword>*, where *<type>* is the category of information you're looking for, such as title or author or subject. So, at the --> prompt, enter *find author birkerts*. You will then see the screen shown in Figure 6.2.

Here are five entries, three of which—those by Sven—seem like pos-sibilities. You are given eight possible commands to type in now. Enter *display long 1* to get a complete (long) listing for entry 1 of the list. Instantly you get the screen shown in Figure 6.3, which looks basically like the card catalog entry for the book, complete with all the informa-tion you'd need if you happened to be in Hanover, New Hampshire, and wanted to check the book out, or if you need to fill out an interlibrary loan request at your own school.

To quit, now type *bye,* and your telnet connection to Dartmouth will be terminated.

If you need to use another computer, somewhere else in the world, telnet is the routine you need. But it's limited to just that—using another

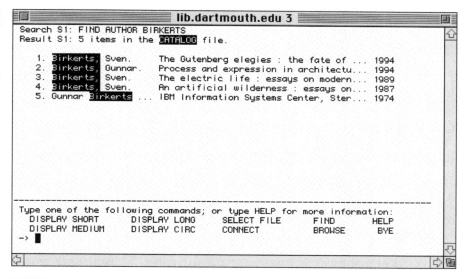

FIGURE 6.2

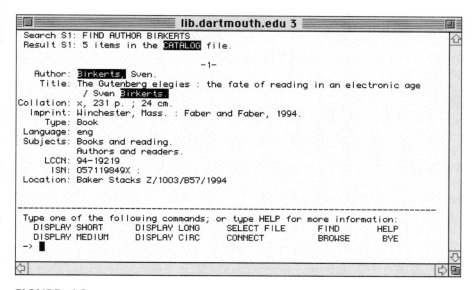

FIGURE 6.3

computer. With pure telnet, you can't copy or retrieve files or information, just display them on your screen.

FTP

File transfer protocol (ftp) is the method the Internet uses to transfer files from one computer to another. The abbreviation, now used as a word, can be either a noun ("retrieve through ftp") or a verb ("to ftp a file"). It's a series of complex instructions (a *protocol*) that computers worldwide use when sending and receiving files so communication among them is possible. When you use ftp, you log onto a remote computer and download the file from that remote computer to your own computer. You need, therefore, access to that remote computer, either by having an account there yourself or by being granted open access as an anonymous user (this is called *anonymous ftp*—by far the most common use of ftp); and you need to know the basic ftp commands (usually those of the most common operating system for mainframe computers connected to the Internet: Unix) for navigating around the remote computer and retrieving the file once you've found it.

Imagine a scenario: there's a file—a text, a picture, maybe even a new piece of software for your computer—that you know about (how you found out is a matter for later treatment!) and want to retrieve for your own. It's stored on a computer somewhere else in the world. How do you get it?

In general, it's a three-step process: first you need to log on to the remote computer, most likely as an anonymous user; second, you need to move around through the various directories and subdirectories until you find the file you're looking for; and third, you need to retrieve the file. (Often there's regrettably a fourth step: with many basic school accounts, when you ftp a file, the file is transferred from the remote computer to your account or volume on your school's mainframe computer, but *not to your own desktop computer*. Hence, you must then go through the additional procedure of downloading that file from your school's computer to your own.)

A Sample FTP

In this case, we'll start with the most primitive assumptions about your Internet connection. You have a dial-up account to your school's Unix-based mainframe computer, which means that your own desktop computer is nothing more than another dumb terminal connected to the mainframe. All commands you issue are first to your school's mainframe and, once you've logged into the remote computer, to that computer. At no time are you actually operating your own computer—commands just pass through it to whatever computer you are logged into.

Let's say you're researching former President Richard Nixon, and have learned that there's a picture of him with Elvis Presley in a directory at the address *<csustan.csustan.edu>*. You're still not quite sure, but it seems at this point that such a picture might be useful in your research paper.

Log onto your own account. At the prompt (most likely a % or perhaps a $), you should be able to type in the command *ftp* followed by a space followed by the address of the computer where your desired file resides:

% ftp csustan.csustan.edu

At this point you see displayed on your screen:

```
220 csustan.csustan.edu FTP server (Version 5.1
(NeXT 1.0) Wed Sep 15, 1993) ready.
Connected to CSUSTAN. CSUSTAN. EDU.
Name (CSUSTAN. CSUSTAN. EDU:<your own login ID>):
```

To login remotely to this anonymous ftp site, at the *Name:* prompt type:

anonymous

You will then see:

```
331 Guest login ok, send ident as password.
Password:
```

At the *Password:* prompt, type your own email address (technically, you don't need any password, but it's netiquette to use your email address). After you type your address, you'll be connected to the remote computer. You'll see the following message.

```
230 Guest login ok, access restrictions apply.
```

At this point you'll see an FTP> prompt; this is where you begin typing commands to the remote computer. In this case, you need to get to the proper directory where your desired picture resides: pub/images/gif/. Type the command *cd* (for "change directory"—one of the few Unix commands that's logical) followed by the name of the directory you want to change to.

```
FTP> cd pub/images/gif
```

Then you see

```
250 CWD command successful.
```

At the next FTP> prompt, type the command to list the contents of the directory, *ls*.

```
FTP> ls
```

Now you will see the following list scroll past on the screen:

```
200 PORT command successful.
150 Opening ASCII mode data connection for file list.
astronaut.gif
bball.gif
best0.gif
best1.gif
best2.gif
bulwnk.gif
elvis-n-nixon.gif
fishy.gif
m51x.gif
moebius.gif
sandman.gif
shuttle15.gif
spaceman.gif
trap1.gif
.cache
.cache+
menu
226 Transfer complete.
183 bytes received in 00:00:00.03 seconds
```

At the FTP> prompt now, type in the command to get the file you want, elvis-n-nixon.gif. The Unix command is *get*.

```
FTP> get elvis-n-nixon.gif
```

You will then see

```
200 PORT command successful.
150 Opening ASCII mode data connection for elvis-n-
nixon.gif
     (244922 bytes).
```

Twenty-one seconds later (actually 21.12 seconds) you will see

```
226 Transfer complete.
local: ELVIS-N-NIXON.GIF remote: elvis-n-nixon.gif
244922 bytes received in 00:00:21.12 seconds
```

Now the file—the picture—is in your account on your school's computer where it probably won't do you much good, unless that's the computer where you do all your writing and printing. More likely, however, you're using your own or your school lab's desktop PC, and you want the picture on a disk so you can use it in your research paper. How do you get it to your own computer? The answer depends on what kind of file it is, and what kind of telecommunications software resources both your PC and your school's mainframe have. The most common and easiest to use is a simple text transfer, and it works fine if the file you're transferring is a simple ASCII text file (just letters and numbers and punctuation, with no formatting such as underlining or fancy quotation marks). If your desktop PC and your host (school's) computer both have Xmodem, Ymodem, Zmodem, or Kermit, you can transfer the file from the host computer to your own using one of those protocols. Most terminal software (ProComm, ZTerm, etc.) offers at least Xmodem, the oldest of the file transfer methods. If your computer's software and your host computer both offer it, use Zmodem. Since procedures for downloading files from host computers to desktop PCs vary so widely, specific instructions can't be give here. If this step gives you trouble, you should contact your school's system administrator for help.

After following these steps, you'll have successfully transferred a file using ftp. Even if you use the fancier graphical ftp programs such as Fetch (on the Macintosh), the procedures are streamlined and automated but essentially the same.

Searching FTP with Archie

Early in the history of the Internet, people realized that ftp was limited because you usually didn't know where to get a file. If someone told you where it was, fine; if not, there was no way to look for a file.

Enter Archie (short for "archiving utility"), developed by Alan Emtage, Peter Deutsch, and Bill Heelan at McGill University to help ftp users find files. It was the first of the spider programs for the Internet. At regular intervals, it crawled over all the anonymous ftp sites it knew about and made a list of their contents, storing that continuously updated list as a giant searchable database. When a user accessed one of the Archie sites (first, by telnet; later, by graphical programs such as Anarchie), she could then perform a keyword search of that database and find out where the information she wanted was available.

This is still the operating principle of Archie: access one of the Archie sites (there are a number of them nowadays, most available via telnet), search the database of ftp sites (using a modified keyword search, described later), then use ftp to access the relevant sites and retrieve the files you want.

Archie actually has a very powerful set of searching tools, despite (or perhaps because of) its heritage as a text-based tool. In its pure text-based incarnations, however, most of Archie's options tend to be so complex and cumbersome as to make it better to simply try another search with new keywords. A few of the simpler commands may help: when you first log on to an Archie site, usually by telnet, you will be informed what the default search is. Normally it's a "case-insensitive substring" search, which means that your search will ignore case and will treat what you've entered as a substring, as if it were both preceded and followed by wildcard characters: searching for *view* would find *viewpoints* and *preview,* for example.

USEFUL UNIX COMMANDS

Unix, being a command-driven operating system, has a huge number of commands. Some of the more useful ones for ftp and telnet sessions are:

apropos	keyword search of all commands
cd	change directory
cp	copy a file
get	retrieve a file though ftp
ls	list files
man	help (short for "manual page")
more	display and scroll a text file
mv	move (or rename!) a file
put	send a file through ftp
rm	delete files

At the Archie> prompt, you can change the type of search. Simply enter *set search* followed by one of the following options:

exact (forces an exact match to what you've entered)

subcase (forces a case-sensitive substring search)

regex (allows the use of a whole range of powerful query construction operators)

It's best not to use regex unless you're an experienced Unix programmer. If you *really* need to construct a complex Archie query, type *help regex* at the Archie> prompt, but don't expect to understand what you get.

Remember, the default is usually *set search sub* (i.e., case-insensitive substring), so you don't need to enter that unless you want to undo an earlier *set search* command.

Once you have the type of search set, you're ready to actually perform the search. At the Archie> prompt, type in *find* followed by the string of characters you want it to look for. The traditional Archie command to institute a search for files was *prog* (don't ask why); thankfully, most Archie servers now allow you to use the more rational *find* command to find files. However, if *find species* (for example) doesn't result in files with the string *species* in them, you'll need to use *prog species*.

After a few seconds or minutes (depending on how complex your search is and how many files Archie finds, you will receive a list of found files and sites where they reside. The results of the above search one day in June were as follows:

```
# Search type: sub, Domain: northamerica.
# Your queue position: 1
# Estimated time for completion: 5 seconds.
working . . .   =O=O=O=

Host ftp.bio.indiana.edu (129.79.225.25)
Last updated 02:57 27 Jun 1996

    Location: /flybase/allied-data
      DIRECTORY drwxrwxr-x 512 bytes 12:30 29 Mar 1996
      species

    Location: /flybase/allied-data/species
      FILE    -rw-rw-r-    218692 bytes        10:30 29 Mar
      1996    species.txt
```

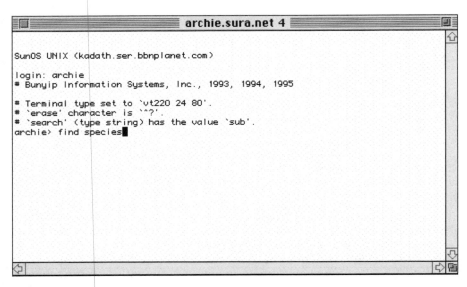

FIGURE 6.4

Location: /flybase/stocks/stock-centers
   FILE   -rw-r-r-   159899 bytes   09:48 10 Jan
   1996   species-center.csv
   FILE   -rw-r-r-   312785 bytes   08:35 10 Jan
   1996   species-center.rpt
   FILE   -rw-r-r-   1508 bytes 15:39 31 Dec 1995
   species-center.doc

Location: /flybase/nomenclature
   FILE   -rw-rw-r-   5929 bytes 20:00 6 Aug 1995
   species-abbreviations.txt

Location: /flybase/docs
   FILE   -rwxrwxrwx 42 bytes   20:00 20 Apr 1995
   stocks-species-center.doc
   FILE   -rwxrwxrwx 26 bytes   20:00 20 Apr 1995
   species.doc

Location: /flybase/allied-data/species
   FILE   -rw-rw-r-   1616 bytes 21:00 4 Dec 1994
   species.doc

```
Location: /flybase/allied-data/DIS
    FILE    -rw-rw-r-   14552 bytes 20:00 16 Oct 1994
    index-species.txt

Location: /flybase/stocks/stock-centers
    FILE    -rw-r-r-    106639 bytes      20:00 2 Jun
    1993    species-center.rtf
```

```
Host sunsite.unc.edu (152.2.254.81)
Last updated 03:46 13 Jun 1996
```

```
Location: /pub/academic/agriculture/agronomy/soil-
chemistry
    DIRECTORY    drwxr-xr-x  512 bytes   20:00 13 Apr
    1993    Species

Location: /pub/academic/agriculture/agronomy/soil-
chemistry/Species
    FILE    -rw-r---    1602088 bytes    20:00 13 Apr
    1993    species.zip
```

```
Host ftp.bio.indiana.edu (129.79.225.25)
    Last updated 02:57 27 Jun 1996
    Location: /flybase/work
    FILE    -rw-rw-r-   2685 bytes  21:00 10 Jan 1993
    species.txt
```

```
archie>
```

Let's analyze what this means. Each two-line entry beginning with Location: is information about a specific file. In the case of the last one,

```
Location: /flybase/work
    FILE    -rw-rw-r-   2685 bytes  21:00 10 Jan 1993
    species.txt
```

the file is located in the directory flybase/work; it's 2685 bytes (bytes are roughly equivalent to letters, it's about 500 words long); it was created January 10, 1993; and its title is *species.txt,* the *.txt* at the end signifying that it's a text file, that is, not a formatted word-processing, graphic, or sound file. The host machine on which the file is found and to which you will need to ftp to get the file is *ftp.bio.indiana.edu.* (Note that in this case, the *ftp* is actually part of the name of the host.) In general, nearly everything else in these entries can be safely ignored by the researcher.

Graphical IP Archie clients such as Anarchie will allow you to search with Archie and retrieve the file directly to your PC in one operation. With text, Archie accessed through telnet, as above, you will need to actually perform a separate ftp operation for each file you want to retrieve.

Limitations of Archie Searches

Archie searches, since they can only search on filenames, depend heavily on the relevance of the name assigned by the creator of the files. A file named *species-abbreviations.txt* is probably a list of the abbreviations of species; a file named *bgf2134.tar* is a mystery file. If your search turns it up, you have no idea what's in it; if you're looking for specific information that is actually found in this file, Archie will not find the file for you because its name is meaningless (at least to most people).

What's Available through FTP

In all honesty, the major use of ftp in the Internet today is probably downloading software packages and utilities for various systems (Macintosh, Windows, Unix, etc.), not a function that you as a researcher would be likely to perform. However, anonymous ftp sites are also sources of text files and documents (particularly government and university research documents), graphics, mailing lists, and Usenet newsgroup archives (see Chapter 4 for an explanation of Usenet archives). Assessing the reliability of information obtained through ftp is normally not a problem; usually ftp sites are maintained by organizations that provide the documents in their finished, evaluated form to the public, so you may judge them as you would any formally published source.

WAIS

WAIS is an acronym for Wide Area Information Server, a set of information storage and retrieval programs developed in the late 1980s. One of the problems with ftp, as you no doubt discovered if you used it much, is that each remote computer you log onto looks different—different commands, different file structures, different files. WAIS was one attempt to bring some order to this chaos of the Internet by providing a way to search all kinds of databases using the same interface and commands, regardless of how the data was organized or where it resided. WAIS has had moderate success at best, never really catching on with the Internet users the way it should have. Perhaps the development of Gopher superseded WAIS before it had a chance. Too bad, in a way; WAIS is actually very powerful.

In any event, WAIS is still a minor player on the Internet and you need to know how to use it. Many times you will find a small site—the federal government still seems to use WAIS quite a bit—using WAIS, and searching that site can actually bring up some surprising and useful information. The future development of WAIS is in limbo as of this writing. It has been purchased by America Online, and many of its resources have temporarily dried up or been withdrawn. America Online has plans for WAIS, but it may or may not be the publicly-accessible worldwide force in information search and retrieval that it seemed destined to be just a few years ago. AOL may revamp it, hype it, and re-introduce it to the Net amidst great fanfare; or, as seems more likely, they may quietly use its resources and routines in the background, so you may be using WAIS frequently in the future without knowing it. Even now, most WAIS searches occur either on local sites or through versions available by Gopher or the WWW. This trend may accelerate in the future but, in the meantime, here's how the current incarnation (pretty much unchanged from 1994 or so) operates.

WAIS in Action

Conducting a WAIS search is a two-step process: you first search a WAIS database that lists all the WAIS servers in the world (well, at least all those who've registered their servers), looking for particular servers that likely will have information that's useful to you. You wouldn't, for example, want to search a NASA WAIS database if you were looking for information on caring for parrots. Once you've found a number of servers of potential value, you conduct an identical search of those servers. With WAIS, once you find an interesting document, you can retrieve it immediately from within the WAIS client. No need to switch applications, to jot down a URL for later use, or to log into an anonymous ftp site and navigate its mysterious files.

WAIS allows, at each step, something called natural language processing. Most researchers in artificial intelligence would dispute the use of this term, but it's close enough. It means that you don't have to construct elaborate queries with strict limitations on how you arrange keywords and what operators you can use. In theory, you can type into the WAIS query box something like "I'm looking for stuff on dinosaurs of the jurassic period" and WAIS will find the right "stuff." In actuality, of course, WAIS is just ignoring common words with little or no content (*I* and *for* and *of*, for example) and performing a keyword fuzzy-AND search on the content words that remain. So WAIS searches the query *dinosaur* AND jurassic AND* *period,* then provides you with a list of of documents from the servers you've searched, and allows you to retrieve any of them immediately.

GOPHER

Gopher's easy-to-use menu interface to the Internet fueled the second Internet revolution. In its heyday—1994 or so—it was wildly popular because it embraced all the current technology (it can do telnet, ftp, and WAIS; so why do you need any of those?) and it was relatively simple to use. It has, in the intervening few years, become less popular as the World Wide Web has risen in popularity. But there's still an enormous amount of information stored on Gopher servers around the world, and while those servers aren't being updated with the regularity of WWW sites, new and useful information continues to appear in gopherspace (the sum total of everything that's available on all the Gopher servers— all 7,500 of them—in the world). Because quite a few gophersites are not being updated, and in many cases are being removed from the Net as the information is transferred to websites, you can expect to meet with a certain amount of frustration because of outdated or missing information, but if you persevere you will encounter material in gopherspace that exists nowhere else on the Internet.

Gopher operates, like much of the Internet, on the client/server principle. Information is stored in a precise format on computers (called servers) and when you open up a client application from or on your own computer, the client software interacts with the server, sending and receiving commands and information. There are SLIP/PPP Gopher clients available for Macintosh and Windows computers, but access to the text-based Gopher client at the University of Minnesota is clean and simple. If you're using your school's text-based dial-in shell account, in all likelihood you can just type the command *gopher* at your prompt and you will be taken either to your school's own Gopher client (very common) or perhaps directly to the Minnesota Gopher. If your school's Gopher client seems to offer a wide range of jumping-off points, use it. If not, it almost certainly will provide a link to the Minnesota Gopher (shown in Figure 6.5).

Every Gopher screen you see will resemble this one—a numbered list of gophersites to access. The gophersites listed in any menu are scattered all over the globe, but you don't know (or need to know) where they are located. That's the beauty and mystery of gopherspace. To choose a site, you can either type its number from the menu or use the up and down arrow keys to move the highlighter (the --> that's currently pointing at *1. Information About Gopher* in Figure 6.5). When you've indicated your choice, press either the Enter key or the right arrow key and you will be

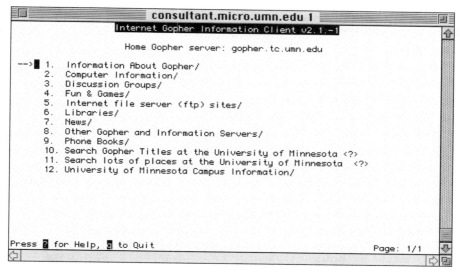

FIGURE 6.5

taken to the site you've chosen. Menu items ending in a slash (/) are directories and will give you another Gopher menu of choices; items ending with <?> are searchable sites. An item with no symbols after it is a document that may be read or downloaded.

If the Gopher list is longer than one screenful, you may access each successive screen with the space bar; you may go back one screen at a time by pressing the *b* key (or the - key). You may go to the previous gophersite (the one where you pressed the right arrow to get where you are) by pressing the left arrow (or the letter *u*—Gopher seems to have a good deal of duplication built in). Gopher contains context-sensitive help—press the *?* key and you'll see a list of helpful commands and instructions relevant to your situation.

Searching Gopherspace with Veronica

Gopher has its own specialized search engine, called Veronica, developed in 1992 at the University of Nevada–Reno. (*Veronica* supposedly stands for *Very Easy Rodent-Oriented Netwide Index to Computer Archives*, but more likely it stands for Archie's girlfriend's name. There also is a limited version of Veronica called Jughead, which supposedly stands for . . . it doesn't matter. You get the picture.) The real beauty of Veronica is that once its search is complete, you can immediately retrieve the files you want without changing software, learning new commands, or copying down an ftp address. Veronica is integrated into Gopher and available from most gophersites. From the Minnesota site shown in Figure 6.5, select item 8, *Other Gopher and Information Servers,* which brings you to another Gopher menu. Choose *Search Titles in Gopherspace Using Veronica,* and you will be presented with the Veronica Gopher menu, shown in Figure 6.6.

Notice items 3–5 (don't ask where items 1 and 2 are) and items 9–11; they seem similar, almost identical, but they are actually the first step in controlling your Veronica search. Both sets give you three different Veronica servers to choose from; if one is busy (a very common occurrence) try another. But items 3, 4, and 5 are searches of Gopher *directories* (those items on Gopher menus followed by slashes). Searching directories results in a much speedier search, since you're searching repositories of documents rather than individual documents themselves.

The other search option—items 9, 10, and 11: *Search Gopherspace by Title Word(s)*—allows a more far-reaching search of all individual documents. This takes longer, of course, but ensures a more thorough search. For both varieties of search, you are dependent on the *names* given to directories and documents; if a name is not descriptive, it won't turn up in your search. A document entitled *Honest_Abe.txt* won't be found when you search using the keywords *Abraham Lincoln.*

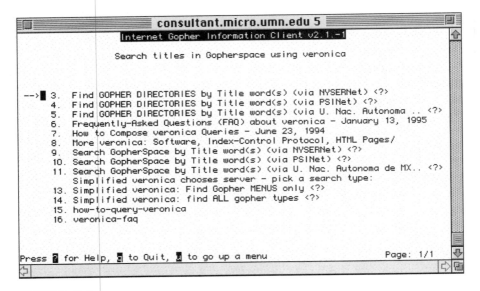

FIGURE 6.6

Veronica uses the keyword search principle. It is actually an extremely precise and powerful search engine, offering a full set of boolean operators and an extensive set of other logicals to construct very precise queries. Select your range of search (directories or titles) and your server by choosing 3, 4, 5, 9, 10, or 11 from the Veronica menu. You will see a screen with a query box (shown in Figure 6.7).

Construct your query by typing it in the box and pressing the Enter key. Help is available with the Control-] command; to abort the query without searching, press control-G. (Another useful command not listed is Control-U. This clears the query box and readies it for a new search.)

Constructing Queries in Veronica

By default, multiple keywords are considered to be boolean AND searches, so that *Abraham Lincoln* and *Abraham AND Lincoln* are equivalent queries. Boolean OR and NOT are available. Veronica searches are not case-sensitive. Veronica queries are read left to right, but the order of operations may be controlled with parentheses. Substring (wildcard) searches are permitted; the wildcard character is * and it may only be used at the end of words.

In addition, you may specify other options for you queries with the modifiers *-t* and *-m*. Adding *-t* to your query restricts your search to *types* of files; some of the more useful types are 0 (text file), 1 (directory), 4

```
┌─────────────────── consultant.micro.umn.edu 5 ───────────────────┐
│                  Internet Gopher Information Client v2.1.-1       │
│                                                                   │
│               Search titles in Gopherspace using veronica        │
│                                                                   │
│                                                                   │
│         3.  Find GOPHER DIRECTORIES by Title word(s) (via NYSERNet) <?> │
│         4.  Find GOPHER DIRECTORIES by Title word(s) (via PSINet) <?> │
│  +───────────Search GopherSpace by Title word(s) (via PSINet)────────────+ │
│  │                                                                   │ │
│  │ Words to search for                                               │ │
│  │                                                                   │ │
│  │ endangered AND species                                            │ │
│  │                                                                   │ │
│  │ [Help: ^-]  [Cancel: ^G]                                          │ │
│  +───────────────────────────────────────────────────────────────────+ │
│        13. Simplified veronica: Find Gopher MENUS only <?>          │
│        14. Simplified veronica: find ALL gopher types <?>          │
│        15. how-to-query-veronica                                   │
│        16. veronica-faq                                            │
│                                                                   │
│ Press ▯ for Help, ▯ to Quit, ▯ to go up a menu        Page: 1/1   │
└───────────────────────────────────────────────────────────────────┘
```

FIGURE 6.7

(Macintosh.hqx file), 5 (PC binary file), 7 (gopher menu), 9 (binary file), s (sound file), I (image other than a.gif file), g (.gif file), and h (.html file). So adding, for example, *-tg* to your query would limit your search to graphics files of type.gif. Normally, Veronica searches display the first 200 found files; you can change that with the *-m* command. If you want to set your maximum number of files displayed to, say, 1,000 instead of 200, just add *-m1000* to your query. Entering nothing after the *-m* will display all files.

So, while Veronica searches are hampered by their inability to examine full texts, it is possible to construct very elaborate and precise queries.

Veronica Search Results

After you enter your query and press the Enter key, Veronica churns for a few moments (watch the ingenious spinning effect generated by an alternation of the /, \, and I text characters!) and returns to you another gopher menu, often multiple screens in length (if it finds 200 items matching your search criteria), this time with sites containing the information you requested. A sample Veronica search with query *Endangered AND Species* generated the first Gopher screen of results (shown in Figure 6.8).

Since Veronica searches only titles and Gopher displays only titles, one of the frustrations of using Gopher is that it's very difficult to tell just what you have when you have a Gopher menu listing only titles.

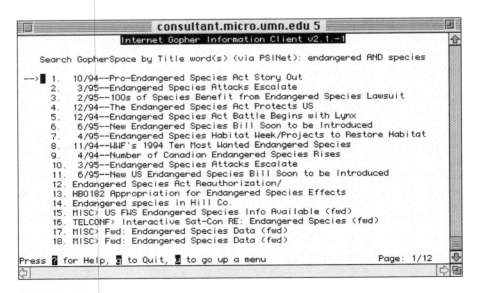

```
┌──────────────────── consultant.micro.umn.edu 5 ────────────────────┐
│               Internet Gopher Information Client v2.1.-1            │
│                                                                    │
│   Search GopherSpace by Title word(s) (via PSINet): endangered AND species
│                                                                    │
│ -->█ 1.   10/94--Pro-Endangered Species Act Story Out             │
│      2.    3/95--Endangered Species Attacks Escalate              │
│      3.    2/95--100s of Species Benefit from Endangered Species Lawsuit
│      4.   12/94--The Endangered Species Act Protects US           │
│      5.   12/94--Endangered Species Act Battle Begins with Lynx   │
│      6.    6/95--New Endangered Species Bill Soon to be Introduced │
│      7.    4/95--Endangered Species Habitat Week/Projects to Restore Habitat
│      8.   11/94--WWF's 1994 Ten Most Wanted Endangered Species    │
│      9.    4/94--Number of Canadian Endangered Species Rises      │
│     10.    3/95--Endangered Species Attacks Escalate              │
│     11.    6/95--New US Endangered Species Bill Soon to be Introduced
│     12. Endangered Species Act Reauthorization/                   │
│     13. HB0182 Appropriation for Endangered Species Effects       │
│     14. Endangered species in Hill Co.                            │
│     15. MISC> US FWS Endangered Species Info Available (fwd)      │
│     16. TELCONF> Interactive Sat-Con RE: Endangered Species (fwd) │
│     17. MISC> Fwd: Endangered Species Data (fwd)                  │
│     18. MISC> Fwd: Endangered Species Data (fwd)                  │
│                                                                    │
│ Press ? for Help, █ to Quit, █ to go up a menu       Page: 1/12   │
└────────────────────────────────────────────────────────────────────┘
```

FIGURE 6.8

Figure 6.8 shows the first 18 items (in no particular order) found as a result of the Veronica search on *Endangered AND Species*. What is contained in these 18 titles is a mystery; use your judgment and select interesting titles for reading. *Some* information is conveyed by this screen, however. This is screen ("page") 1 and there are 12 total, meaning 200 items are displayed and in all likelihood more are waiting to be displayed. If you want to see more than 200 items, redo the search changing the maximum number displayed with the -m operator. Help is available (the ? key), and two useful commands are noted as reminders: *q* to quit and *u* to go up a screen (not possible on screen 1). Scroll forward screen by screen with the space bar, making choices with the arrow keys, moving to a document with the right arrow and returning with the left arrow. Somewhere in these menus lies a good amount of useful information, usually.

What You Can Find in Gopherspace

Gopher's real strength is its fast text-based menu interface, so it's popular with people with slow modem connections who can't wait for the glitz of webpages to be downloaded. As noted above, gopherspace lies in a bit of disrepair, suffering from some neglect. Its major value is storing text and images, because the text and image files don't need to be modified as they do for display on the web. If someone has a simple text document—a report, compilation of data, or narrative—it's a simple matter to store it unaltered on a Gopher server. The complete government text of the Endangered Species Act of 1973 is available through Gopher, for example, as are thousands of classical literary texts (all of Shakespeare) and tens of thousands of organizations' documents.

Another popular use of Gopher is a CWIS (Campus Wide Information Service). Many colleges and universities have gathered campus information —faculty offices and phone numbers, lists of administrators, library holdings, sometimes even the whole college course catalog—and placed it on a CWIS Gopher server. Anyone can then quickly and easily find answers to questions about the college simply by accessing the CWIS.

One mixed blessing of a Veronica search is the practice of storing listserv and Usenet (see Chapter 4) archives on Gopher servers. On one hand, this is a convenient way to access stored messages and entire threads of earlier online discussions; on the other hand, often what turns up in a Veronica search is many, many isolated, decontextualized messages—questions with no answers, answers with no questions, comments with no frame of reference provided. This is frustrating to the researcher, because a lot of noise in the form of these eerie ghosts of conversations distracts from the focus of a Veronica search. Few things are more frustrating than spotting a title that looks stunningly useful in a Gopher menu, only to find that it's an old Usenet posting from three years ago consisting in its entirety of the words "I agree!" This happens more frequently than you'd ever expect.

Finally, because Gopher is a later technology than ftp, telnet, and WAIS, it encompasses all of those. When you're navigating gopherspace, sliding from state to state and country to country, searching for and retrieving files from who knows where, you're actually doing telnet, ftp, and WAIS, but all those processes are invisible, in the background, silent.

FINAL WORDS

If you're at all familiar with the World Wide Web, tunneling through gopherspace with a text-based Gopher client may seem like poking about in someone's attic—it's dusty and uncared for, in many ways, but there are still treasures to be found. And doing a text-based ftp can seem like searching a hundred-year-old barn that collapsed fifty years ago.

With the increase in popularity and accessibility of SLIP/PPP Internet connections, new graphical software for ftp, WAIS, and Gopher has popped up. IP clients like TurboGopher for the Macintosh or Hgopher for Windows take all the pain and fuss out of the older technologies. How easy it is now to point and click or drag and drop your way through an ftp session with Anarchie, a graphical Archie-search-and-ftp-retrieve application. In current practice, if you have access to the World Wide Web with a graphical IP browser, you will be able to do everything described in this chapter quickly and easily, without ever changing software. Netscape and Mosaic can do everything here.

EXERCISES

1. Use Archie to find ftp sites where information on alcoholism is stored. How much information is there? How up-to-date is it? When was the most recent document added? What compression and/or conversion types are represented? Which ones can you decode with the software and hardware you now have? (You may have to check with your school's system operator to answer this fully.)

2. Using ftp, download one of the files. Can you decode it into a usable file?

3. Use Veronica to find the same file. Download it. What differences do you notice between Gopher and ftp?

4. What are your personal criteria for evaluating the validity of information you obtain from these sources? How do you tell when information is biased or simply wrong?

5. How does misinformation get onto the Internet?

7

COMMERCIAL ON-LINE SERVICES

Technically speaking, commercial on-line services such as America Online (AOL) and CompuServe (CIS) are not part of the Internet. But they are very popular sources of on-line information (America Online boasts of just having passed six million subscribers as of this writing), some of which is not available on the Internet itself. If you have an account on one of the services, you should learn how to search them and find the information they have to offer, for despite their ease of use, they are still thickets of relatively disorganized information. Both are set up to encourage browsing rather than searching, so locating and retrieving specific information efficiently is difficult. Neither CompuServe nor America Online offers a service-wide full-text search mechanism; their global search functions only return a list of suggested areas for exploration, but not specific files or documents.

Throughout the explosive growth of the on-line services in recent years, it has become fashionable among Internet veterans to disparage these services. In fact, the more Net-savvy you become, the more likely it is you will gravitate toward a direct IP (SLIP or PPP) Internet connection yourself. But despite the bad-mouthing by the old guard, most of whom long for the days when they and about a thousand other people had the Internet all to themselves, there are a number of advantages to using America Online or CompuServe for your Net research, particularly if you're a relative beginner on the Net.

First, both AOL and CIS are easy to set up, and you get a full graphical interface without going through the complicated processes necessary to set up your own SLIP/PPP connection. SLIP and PPP systems are notoriously difficult and quirky to set up. Both AOL and CIS provide you with full (well, almost full) access to the entire Internet—ftp, Gopher, and the

WWW, though as of this writing neither provides IRC, and AOL does not offer telnet capability.

Second, in addition to Internet access, you get access to all the proprietary materials on the service—databases, research and news services, libraries of software and graphics, and so forth. Some of these materials are actually owned and operated by the service itself (such as forums for teachers or motorcyclists), and some are subscription services (such as *Time* magazine, *U.S. News,* and encyclopedias) which AOL and CompuServe make available to their users. Both offer limited chat rooms, similar to IRC but restricted to other subscribers of the service. Because you pay for these on-line services, you get more from them. Some of the material is marginally useful for research—on-line encyclopedias and dictionaries, for example. But there is an ever-expanding foundation of proprietary or limited-access databases available in each service.

The greatest disadvantage of these services is the monthly bill that starts at $9.95 and rises rapidly, depending on how much time you stay on line and, in the case of CompuServe, how many of the premium services you access, racking up additional hourly charges and per-piece fees paid to outside search services ($1.00 for each search of CIS's on-line *Book Review Digest,* for example, and an additional fixed price for each review you find that you want to download and read). One irony is that this disadvantage may actually turn out to be an advantage, for though the Internet is a living rejection of the cliché "you get what you pay for" (with the Internet you often pay nothing but get huge benefits), by subscribing to one of these commercial services you actually have access to more information. There are times when even CompuServe's maddening pricing policies work to your benefit, as you can search databases that are not available to the general Net surfer. You do need to keep careful tabs on your use of their premium services, however, or you can easily run up a bill of $100 or $200 per month.

One final note—owing to their overwhelming popularity, only America Online and CompuServe are discussed in this chapter. While smaller services of note continue to exist—GEnie, Prodigy, Delphi, to name the best known—it's likely that if you subscribe to a commercial on-line service, you subscribe to either America Online or Compuserve. All the on-line services offer similar functions, and if you subscribe to a different one, you can easily adapt the advice that follows to the particulars of your service.

AMERICA ONLINE (AOL)

America Online was the first national on-line service to recognize the value of graphical interfaces and has thus become the largest service. It offers Internet access with its graphical interface, allowing you to simply, quickly, and intuitively perform ftp, Gopher, and Web functions. The price you pay (besides the monetary one) is in relative slowness, but AOL performs all its Internet functions with *adequate* speed.

The Internet with AOL

It's important to remember that everything discussed in the earlier chapters (with the exception of telnet) is available via AOL. You can do Archie searches and anonymous ftp transfers. You can do WAIS and Gopher (in fact, one of the small number of Veronica servers left in the world is AOL's, and it's actually more accessible and faster than the other publicly available Veronica servers). You can browse the Web with AOL's webbrowser—not as full-featured as Netscape or Mosaic, but nevertheless serviceable. And although AOL has bought WebCrawler and expanded it into one of the major Web search engines, you also can do AltaVista or Infoseek searches. You have a good (if not perfect) email utility, and access to Usenet with, once again, a good but not perfect newsreader utility.

But there are a few quirks and differences to AOL's approach to the Net that need pointing out. First, AOL combines its WAIS and Veronica searches into one service, so you don't really know whether, at any given time, you're searching a WAIS database or a Veronica server. When you click on the Internet Connection from the main Channels screen, you see the screen shown in Figure 7.1

Here you have a number of options, but the obvious ones (and most useful to the researcher) are the graphical icons for World Wide Web, Gopher & WAIS, FTP, and News Groups (Help is available by clicking on the FAQ icon). Clicking on the World Wide Web icon opens the AOL Web Browser and takes you to the AOL Home Page on the web. The Gopher & WAIS icon takes you to the screen shown in Figure 7.2.

The selectable icons (Search, Gopher Directory, What is Gopher, and Help) are all straightforward. The Search icon allows you to perform a Veronica search with the AOL webbrowser. It takes you to AOL's own Veronica server, which is usually less busy than others on the Internet. If it's consistently busy, or not working properly, then click on Gopher Directory and go to the main gopherserver at the University of Minnesota (see Chapter 6). Either way, performing a Veronica search brings up a query box (shown in Figure 7.3).

You can set the number of hits and choose between a default substring search ("partially") or an exact match. Type your keywords (boolean AND is the default link between consecutive terms; other boolean operators are not possible in the AOL Veronica). If you need to construct more complex queries, choose the Gopher Directories option instead, which, despite its misleading name, actually offers you access to the

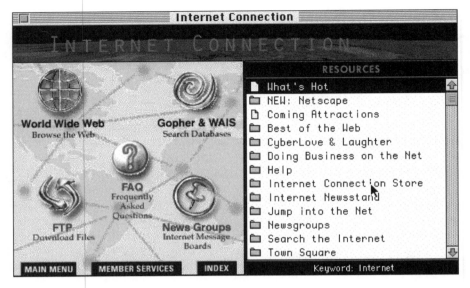

FIGURE 7.1

FIGURE 7.2

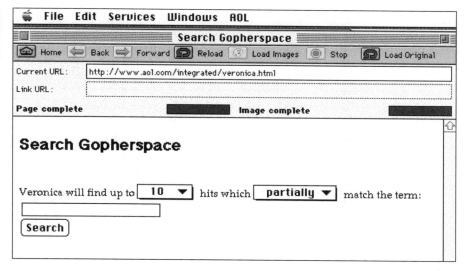

FIGURE 7.3

University of Minnesota Gopher and allows for Veronica searches of titles as well as directories. See Chapter 6 for more information on the University of Minnesota Gopher site.

America Online Proprietary Services

America Online's services come in three flavors: forums (also called, confusingly, *areas, clubs,* or even *roundtables*), chat rooms, and message boards. These are arranged initially for browsing into twenty-one Channels, shown on the opening screen (Figure 7.4).

Clicking on any one of the channels' icons takes you there, where you will be presented with an array of icons and usually a listing of that department's contents. The contents of each channel vary, but with the exception of "People Connection" all will offer you a series of forums, message boards, and chat rooms. (*People Connection* is the gateway to AOL's open chat rooms.) Many of the forums are further subdivided into subforums, message boards, and chats.

Forums

Forums are loosely-organized topical groupings of information. Within a forum you are likely to find further divisions and services—other

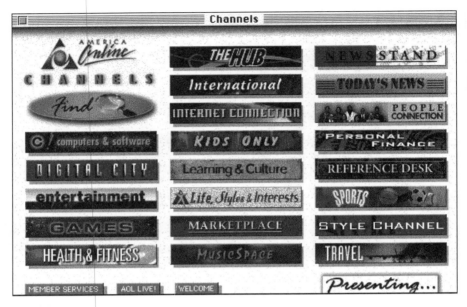

FIGURE 7.4

forums, chat rooms, databases, proprietary services, message boards (similar to Usenet newsgroups, but available only to AOL subscribers), software libraries, and so on. Each forum has its own keyword associated with it, so that if you use a particular forum frequently, you will probably remember its keyword for a shortcut. To jump to a specific forum, click on the keyword button in the menu bar or choose "keyword" from the Go To menu. You will be presented with an entry box (see Figure 7.5). Type the exact keyword and you will be transported to that forum. A kind of search is also available at this screen. A list of acceptable keywords is available by typing *keyword* at the keyword entry box (got that?). Currently, there are over 5,000 keywords available—far too many to memorize.

Searching AOL

Pinpointing a specific piece of information in AOL is likely to be a frustrating process, because it's set up for browsing instead. If you know the general area (channel) your topic is likely to reside in, you can click on its icon at the Channels screen and go there to begin browsing through the various forums until you find (or don't find) what you're looking for.

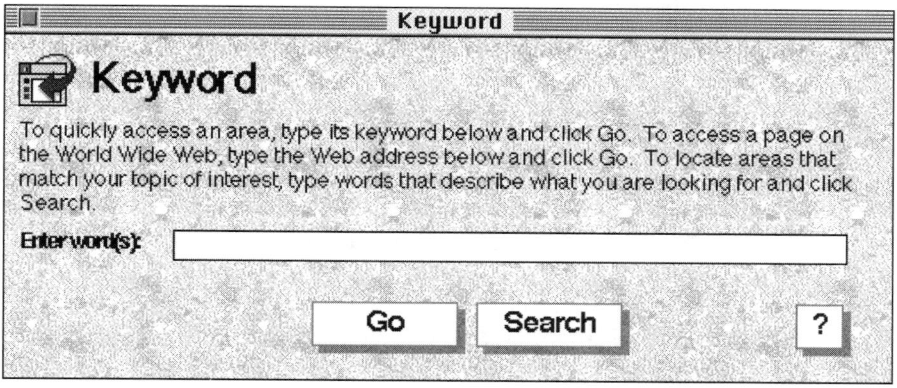

FIGURE 7.5

If you need to search for information, however, you have some options and a fairly complex set of procedures to go through.

First, there are no fewer than four types of Find operations available: a global AOL Find, a software search, a search for keywords (not to be confused with a keyword search), and a Channel Find for each channel.

The global AOL search actually just scans the AOL Directory, a list of all the services and forum areas along with their associated topics. The AOL Search allows for boolean queries (AND, OR, and NOT) but no other logical operators. In general, precise searches aren't needed because the database you're searching is so small. The result of this kind of search is a list of forums which may contain information about your topic. You then must go to that forum and search again, this time using an index of areas or choosing from a small set of icons for especially popular services.

The AOL Find search adds a Search the Internet option as the final item of all hitlists it returns to you. This option sends you to the AOL web-browser and the WebCrawler search engine, which AOL has purchased. From there you can proceed to search the WWW as with any search engine (see Chapter 5).

Channel Find is actually a browser rather than a search engine of any sort. From any of the channels' main screens, choosing FIND brings up a list of all forums and services in that channel, sorted either alphabetically by name or by topic. Either way, you must scroll through the list and find a forum that looks promising, then choose that forum and continue browsing and choosing until you work your way down to the document you want, if it exists.

The keyword entry screen also allows a search of sorts. If you don't know the appropriate keyword from the list of 5,000, you have the option of selecting Search rather than Go (see Figure 7.5).

Selecting Search initiates a keyword search to find forums associated with your query (again, you have the option of constructing a boolean phrase). You will be presented with a hitlist of forums and services that are relevant to your search, although the database you search seems to be the AOL directory again, so if your query phrase is not an existing keyword or some form of one, you aren't likely to find anything. Once the search has finished, you may select any item on your hitlist to go there, where you will need to browse through directories and indexes to find the actual documents you want.

Throughout its maze of different search functions, AOL makes locating a particular bit of information or document difficult with its lack of a true global, full-text search capability. Exploring and browsing are its strengths—it takes perseverance to find something if you know what you're looking for.

COMPUSERVE INFORMATION SERVICE (CIS)

Originally a text-based service, CompuServe lost its lead as the most popular commercial on-line service, but is rebuilding its reputation with a new graphical interface (called the CompuServe Information Manager, or CIM) and a number of new services. Like America Online, CompuServe offers access to a wide range of Internet functions—ftp, Usenet, and email. Unlike AOL, CompuServe offers the telnet service. There is, however, no built-in Gopher or WAIS service, and web browsing is available only for Windows machines. (By the time you read this, the web browser should be available for Macintosh computers.) In the meantime, CIS allows you to use it as a PPP provider, which lets you use your favorite browser such as Netscape and other utilities for Gopher and WAIS—a handy option when you're out of range of your school or your regular ISP. If you're vacationing in Fort Lauderdale and want to check your email back at school or browse the Web for a while, you can do it with CompuServe without a long distance call.

When you first connect to CompuServe, you see the screen shown in Figure 7.6.

Like America Online, CompuServe suggests a number of top-level departments—in this case fifteen, plus the generic Member Service department—to begin your browsing. Each of the icons allows you to burrow deeper and deeper into the contents indicated by the heading until you eventually reach a list of forums and other contents. If you

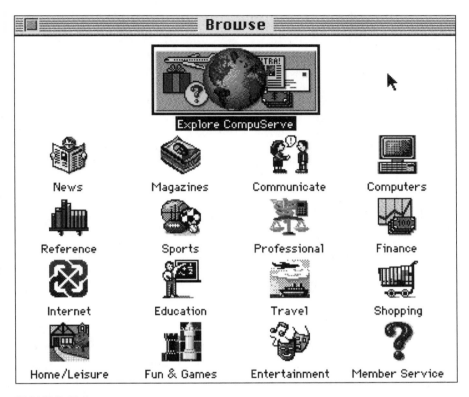

FIGURE 7.6

have some idea of what subject heading your topic might fall under, you can browse CompuServe in this way, and just as with browsing the WWW sites, you often will come up with useful and surprising information. But more likely, you'll want to conduct a search of CompuServe; doing this is discussed later.

The Internet with CompuServe

CompuServe offers ftp, Usenet, and email service built into its software, and by the time you read this it will have a web browser integrated into the package. Since it offers a text-based telnet service through its terminal emulation mode, it theoretically can offer you Gopher and WAIS as well, though you must jump off from the actual CompuServe service to access them.

Thanks to the graphical interface of CIM, CompuServe simplifies ftp—it even offers a preliminary list of anonymous ftp sites to get you started. Unfortunately, it has no built-in search engine, so you have to tel-net to one of the Archie sites, find the ftp sites that have the files or infor-mation you need, and go back to the CompuServe ftp function to retrieve them. The interface is nominally graphical, but it shows its text-based roots, resembling a Unix command-line interface with a few clickable buttons more than a true graphical interface. However, it does allow for navigating the directories of an anonymous ftp site, albeit somewhat clumsily, and for downloading files directly to your desktop PC.

The email and Usenet newsreader functions are serviceable. Both offer standard features such as replying to messages, creating new mes-sages and posts, and saving the messages for future reference. One glar-ing omission: there is no way to search Usenet from within CompuServe. This means you need to go out into the Internet through telnet or a web browser in order to access DejaNews or some of the other Usenet archives. You may subscribe to and participate in listservs comfortably with the CompuServe mail utility.

CompuServe Forums

The concept of a forum is the same in CompuServe and America Online—an on-line collection of related message boards, libraries and databases, and real-time conferences gathered around a particular topic. Examples of CompuServe forum topics are SCUBA, diabetes, and the UK. To take full advantage of the forums, normally you have to become a member of that forum, but this is usually just a formality, costing noth-ing extra and requiring a mere mouseclick to join.

Once you're a member of a forum, you can read the messages (simi-lar to Usenet messages, except on a smaller scale), post your own mes-sages, browse the file libraries, and participate in real-time conferences with other members of the forum. In the libraries of the UK Forum, for example, you can find a listing of the tax rates for the United Kingdom for the current year. Individual forum libraries are searchable.

Searching CompuServe

CompuServe's CIM offers a less-than-ideal approach to searching. For text and information contained in the forum libraries, you need to go through a two-step process similar to a WAIS search: first, you need to perform a Find from either the Services menu or the floating menu bar "find" icon (it looks like a magnifying glass). Fill in the query box pre-sented with one or more keywords. Searches are simple boolean AND searches—no other boolean or other operators are available. The result of this Find is a list of forum sites where your keywords may be found. Then you need to go to the forums indicated, one by one (if more than one is indicated) and perform another search by pulling down the Libraries menu and selecting Search.

You have three options, as shown in Figure 7.7, which is a search of the Animals forum: search by filename, by user ID, and by keywords. It's not likely you'll know the name of a specific file or the user ID of a promising contributor of files, so your best choice will be to search by keyword. Again, the only kind of search permitted is a simple boolean AND search. The default time period indicated is Since [Your] Last Visit, which you will want to change to a much longer period of time. Clicking on the button that reads 1/1/80 brings up a calendar that allows you to specify the time range of files you will accept; you may want to leave it at 1/1/80. By default, all the topical databases within the forum are selected to be searched; if you want to exclude a particular database for some reason, you may click on it to deselect it. When you have your query constructed, click on the Search button or press the Enter key. You will be presented with a list of files that meet your search criteria. You may view the ones that look promising, or you may go straight to downloading them to your computer before viewing.

Searching for files and graphics is also tricky. You need to choose a particular searcher (CompuServe calls them *file finders*) based on the kind of information you're looking for, and employ one of those searchers. As

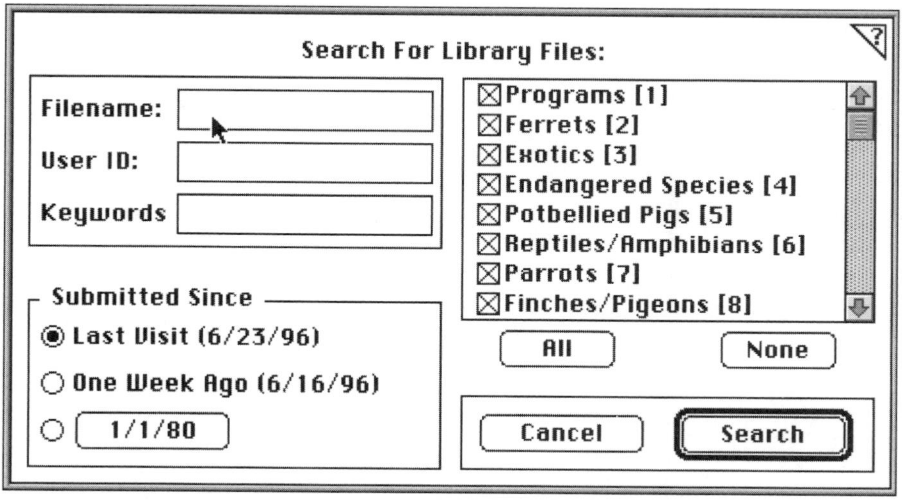

FIGURE 7.7

of this writing, the topical file finders are Adult, Amiga, Games, Graphics, Macintosh, Microsoft, Novell, PC, and Windows. Each of these file finders works identically to the global Find service, but their search fields are limited to certain forums indicated by their names; e.g., the graphics finder only searches the graphics libraries. You will probably find that, because these are more strictly limited almost entirely to binary files (software applications and graphics), these will be of less use to you.

EXERCISES

1. Find all the information you can on *arthritis* on America Online. How does it compare with what you find by searching the Web?

2. Do the same with CompuServe. What differences do you notice?

3. Explain what advantages there may be to using a commercial on-line service instead of the Internet itself.

4. Make a list of the different searches you can conduct in America Online. How many are there?

5. In what ways is the America Online web browser similar to the one you normally use? In what ways is it different? If you use the Windows version of CompuServe, compare its web browser to your own.

8

SPECIALIZED INTERNET SOURCES

SUPER-SITES

So far, we've covered general Internet searches for finding information anywhere on the Net. But there are some specialized sources of information, similar to the proprietary sources in America Online and Compu-Serve, that you should know about. The information available in these sources is, for the most part, still findable through the regular searches described in earlier chapters, and many of them are referenced on major directories such as Yahoo, but knowing about the interesting and useful mega-sites on the Internet described in this chapter may shave some time off your searches.

Most of these sites are on the Web, although some offer their information in less splashy Gopher and ftp formats for those of you who don't have access to the Web or prefer not to wait for the graphics of the Web to trickle in. All are central repositories of hundreds or thousands of links to topical information or resources. Some of the following sites are searchable; some provide links to other specialized sites around the world.

Let's start with the big one(s): the U.S. federal government. Nearly every branch of the federal government has an Internet presence, with well-designed webpages and deep reservoirs of Gopher- and WAIS-based information. (If you've been surfing the Net for long, you already know that you can send the President email, if you want.) Each site may be accessed individually, but there are two super-indexes of government Net resources: the *U.S. Federal Government Agencies* (http://winslo.ohio. gov/fdgvtop.html) and *WWW Servers (U.S. Federal Government)* (http:// sdf.laafb.af.mil/us_gov.html). These will lead you to just about anywhere in the information archives of the government, one of the world's largest purveyors of information.

Some government sites you may want to jump to directly, depending on your topic and interests, are *Thomas: Legislative Information on the Internet* (http://thomas.loc.gov/), named after Jefferson, not Clarence. *Thomas* contains the full text of all legislation and proposed legislation before the House of Representatives and the Senate dating back to the 103rd Congress, plus a keyword search of the full text of *The Congressional Record*. The second is the *Census Bureau Home Page* (http://www.census.gov/), with all the statistics about the American population you'd ever want to know. Although not a government-sponsored site, the *United States Supreme Court Decisions* site (http://www.law.cornell.edu/supct/supct.table.html) at Cornell University is useful for the texts of Supreme Court decisions since 1990 (and most important pre-1990 decisions); it is keyword searchable and updated within one day of the handing down of a decision. NASA was one of the first governmental agencies to jump onto the Internet, since its charter (and therefore its funding and its existence) demands that it disseminate its findings widely; the *NASA Spacelink* is found at http://spacelink.msfc.nasa.gov/. Both the Library of Congress (http://lcweb.loc.gov/homepage/lchp.html) and the Smithsonian Institute (http://www.si.edu/) have websites, but they are actually disappointing if you're expecting huge repositories of substantial information. They are more guides to the actual Washington, D.C., institutions rather than on-line versions of those institutions. If you want to know the hours of the Science and Technology Reading Room at the Library of Congress, you can find it here; if you want to read a book from there, you're out of luck. Maybe some day. . . .

For current affairs and up-to-the-minute information, *Time* magazine is on line, (http://www.timeinc.com/time/), but even better, bigger, and splashier is the awe-inspiring CNN website at http://www.cnn.com/. If it's happened recently, CNN has covered it, and their website will have complete coverage in text, sound, pictures, and video, along with enough sidebars and other perspectives to keep any info-junkie happy.

The one drawback to the CNN site is that it seems to have a short memory. Information from a month or a year ago that once was displayed prominently, seems to disappear. A full cumulative archive of all the info that's ever appeared on this site would make sense, but after a story disappears from the headlines, all associated materials disappear from the CNN site. There is a "vault" of information, but it's clearly not a full archive.

More generic mega-sites include the Internet Public Library (http://www.ipl.org/), as close as you can come in cyberspace to browsing your own bricks-and-mortar library—a jumping off point to Net resources on just about every topic you can imagine (Figure 8.1).

FIGURE 8.1

Also, if you want to pick the brains of the best scholars in the world, you might try the World Lecture Hall (http://wwwhost.cc.utexas.edu/world/lecture/), a compendium of syllabi and supplementary resources from hundred of teachers worldwide who teach courses on line. Here you can see what the professionals recommend. The British Library is also on line (http://portico.bl.uk), with the same limitations as the Library of Congress, but it's still useful for browsing.

More focused super-sites are the humanities collections *Institute for Advanced Technology in the Humanities WWW Server* (http://jefferson.village.virginia.edu/) and *The Voice of the Shuttle* (http://humanitas.ucsb.edu/humanitas_home.html); the English Literature page on *The Voice of the Shuttle* (http://humanitas.ucsb.edu/shuttle/english.html) is particularly useful if you're researching a literary topic. Education (and all that includes) is researchable through the on-line version of the famous ERIC database (http://ericir.syr.edu/), though again, sadly, full-text retrieval of the documents it includes is not yet available, though promised. You'll have to settle for texts of a number of excellent digests (overviews) of specialized topics and go to your real-world librarian to request the documents you've found through searching the on-line ERIC database.

One of the oldest chestnuts on the Internet is still (surprisingly) up-to-date, fresh, and valuable. Gopher-jewels (gopher://cwis.usc.edu:70/11/Other_Gophers_and_Information_Resources/Gopher-Jewels) has been around forever, in Internet years. But it's one of the most complete collections of Gopher sites on the Net. Like Yahoo on the Web, Gopher-jewels arranges its sites hierarchically, the top-level categories being shown in Figure 8.2.

Since these are all gophersites, the material you're likely to find will be text-based, so it will be informative and will download quickly. To be sure, in keeping with current trends, many of the gophersites listed are also available as websites with basically the same information, but if it's pure text-based information you're after, Gopher-jewels may be a good place to start browsing. Gopher-jewels also includes a minimal search engine, allowing you to search its Gopher subdirectories, but since everything is organized logically and hierarchically, it's easy enough to find an appropriate gophersite quickly.

Finally, some specialized sites that may also provide a shortcut to specific information: *The Internet Movie Database* (http://us.imdb.com/) —everything you ever wanted to know about any movie, actor, actress, or director; The U.S. Department of Agriculture Economics and Statistics Gopher server (gopher://usda.mannlib.cornell.edu/1); *The Sheffield ChemDex,* an extensive list of Chemistry Internet sites (http://www.shef.ac.uk/uni/academic/A-C/chem/chemistry-www-sites.html); the *National Data Archive on Child Abuse and Neglect* (http://www.ndacan.cornell.edu);

```
               Internet Gopher Information Client v2.1.3

                          Gopher-Jewels

  --->█ 1.   GOPHER JEWELS Information and Help/
        2.   Community, Global and Environmental/
        3.   Education, Social Sciences, Arts & Humanities/
        4.   Economics, Business and Store Fronts/
        5.   Engineering and Industrial Applications/
        6.   Government/
        7.   Health, Medical, and Disability/
        8.   Internet and Computer Related Resources/
        9.   Law/
       10.   Library, Reference, and News/
       11.   Miscellaneous Items/
       12.   Natural Sciences including Mathematics/
       13.   Personal Development and Recreation/
       14.   Research, Technology Transfer and Grants Opportunities/
       15.   Search Gopher Jewels Menus by Key Word(s) <?>



 Press ? for Help, q to Quit, u to go up a menu              Page: 1/1
```

FIGURE 8.2

the *National Clearinghouse for Alcohol and Drug Information* (http://www.health.org/); and *A Collection of Computer Science Bibliographies* (http://liinwww.ira.uka.de/bibliography/index.html), which actually provides links to thousands of full texts in many instances.

PAY-PER-SEARCH SITES

More and more frequently, companies are realizing that there's money to be made on the Internet, and fee-based information services are popping up. Many of these are very expensive (costing as much as $120 per hour plus a charge for each document found!) but because they are commercial-grade services and will do much of the searching for you, they may be of some value under certain conditions. In many cases, your library may subscribe to a number of the major services and may actually pay the fees for you. It's worth investigating.

Dialog

The great grandaddy of on-line library search services, Dialog, is now available over the Internet via telnet (dialog.com). Dialog specializes in news- and business-related data, but it's a mammoth source of information, including newswire services, newspapers, Dun & Bradstreet,

Standard & Poor, and more. (For a mere $30 per *minute* you can search the TRW Business Credit Profiles.) To check out the Dialog service, see the informational website at http://www.dialog.com.

Lexis-Nexis

Lexis-Nexis, another of the major research services that predates the Internet, is now available on line. Lexis is one of the major repositories of legal information, indexing federal and state laws and case briefs. Nexis indexes news. Lexis-Nexis may be available for free through your library; if not, you may access it by telnetting to lex.meaddata.com. Information on the Internet version of Lexis-Nexis is available on the website at http://www.lexisnexis.com.

Dow Jones News/Retrieval

Strictly business, Dow Jones News/Retrieval (http://bis.dowjones.com/index.html) is an enormous source of business and economic data, particularly current and even up to the minute information such as stock quotes, etc. It carries the text of the *Wall Street Journal,* the *New York Times,* the *Washington Post,* and many other major dailies. The *Wall Street Journal* is even carried in an interactive version. Dow Jones News/Retrieval claims to index and provide full-text retrieval of over 3,400 publications. All for a price, of course.

ClariNet

ClariNet is actually a subset of Usenet. It's one of the few sources of real news on Usenet. Clarinet offers newsfeeds from United Press International and computer-related news from *Newsbytes.* It's a fee-based subscription service, but often, the subscription fee is picked up by your school or ISP, so, if your school or ISP provides the ClariNet service, you can use it for free. ClariNet newsgroups are indicated by having a top-level domain of *clari.* Like other Usenet groups, Clarinet groups are organized hierarchically, clari.news being general news, clari.biz being business news, etc.

NlightN

Despite having perhaps the worst name on the Internet, NlightN (http://www.nlightn.com/) is an amazingly useful tool, gathering together a massive worldwide index of indexes. It offers access to abstracts, indexes, libraries, the *Reader's Guide to Periodical Literature,* and literally hundreds more—all in one universal search. You can search for free, with a complete set of boolean operators available for your queries, and then purchase the found items directly while still on line. Many whole-text documents are available for on line instant delivery; some are sent by U.S. mail or fax. If you have a credit card with a big limit, this is the service for researching from the comfort of your own room.

Cognito

Cognito (http://wwwqa.cognito.com/) (Figure 8.3) is a student-oriented service along the lines of NlightN. It doesn't index as many sources and journals, but its flat $9.95 per month fee for unlimited access to documents is attractive. It includes 700 periodicals, along with the usual collection of encyclopedias, dictionaries, and other desk-reference resources for searching. It also offers a free one-month trial subscription.

The Electric Library

The Electric Library (http://www.elibrary.com) is another family- and student-oriented subscription document retrieval service. It offers a large database of articles and resources (supposedly a billion words and 900 full-text periodicals, for example) updated daily. It features a natural language search interface—queries are entered as English sentences, and the engine translates the sentence into a search query. There is no need for boolean phrase queries.

EasyNet 2.0

EasyNet 2.0 is a professional data search service; information, subscription details, and pricing are available at http://www.telebase.com/easynet.htm. It is a pay-by-document service, with a large database of resources for searching, especially strong in business and economics. It requires special software, available for both Windows and Macintosh, but the software is free.

UnCover

UnCover was one of the earliest on-line document search and retrieval services, and its interface shows it. It uses a text-based telnet connection (*telnet database.carl.org*), but the interface at all points offers plenty of help, and all interactions are conducted by menu choice, so it's not unusually difficult. You search the UnCover database (which includes periodical articles from around 1988 on), and when you find one or more you want, you mark them for ordering. Instructions for payment are included, and

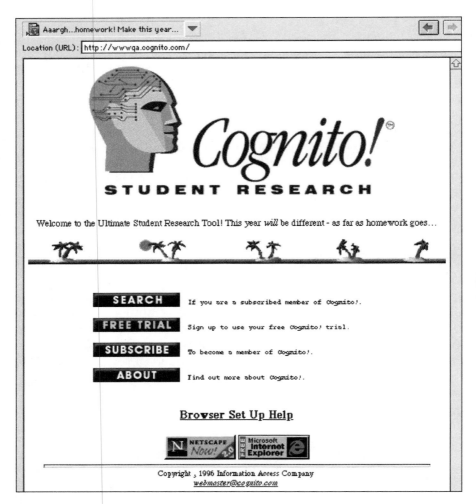

FIGURE 8.3

the ordered documents are faxed to you (yes, you need access to a fax machine) within 24 hours. Prices start at $8.50 per document, plus copyright fees (if any) and additional fees for unusual faxing demands.

Encyclopedia Britannica Online

An Encyclopedia Britannica Online (http://www.eb.com/) subscription costs $150 per year. Enough said.

9

WRITING THE PAPER

EVALUATING AND USING SOURCES

Now that you've seen the process of finding and getting the information, let's look at the process in action—how to evaluate your sources and information and use them in your paper. A series of Gopher, ftp, Usenet, and WWW searches turns up a long list of possible resources. Of what value are they, and how can they be used as evidence for your assertions in your paper?

The writer of this paper has been following the Endangered Species Act, wondering how effective it has been. He first checks the Web with AltaVista. Using the simple query +"*Endangered Species Act*" +*effective* gives the screen shown in Figure 9.1.

Note that *AltaVista* finds about 1,000 sites that may be relevant, and, as always, rank-orders them in terms of relevance. It may be worthwhile to check out the first three or four pages of results, but after that the pages become marginally relevant at best. But there is potential here: the item *Improving the Endangered Species Act* seems focused directly on the issue at hand, and a number of other items on this and the next few pages seem promising as well.

Let's look at the first one, *Improving the Endangered Species Act*. Retrieving it shows it was reprinted from the *Endangered Species Bulletin* Vol. XX No. 3, and is essentially a news item reporting the changes in the ESA recommended by the Secretary of the Interior. It begins with the calm announcement, "Ten principles to improve implementation of the Endangered Species Act (ESA) were announced last spring by Interior Secretary Bruce Babbitt and Dr. D. James Baker, Undersecretary of Commerce." It

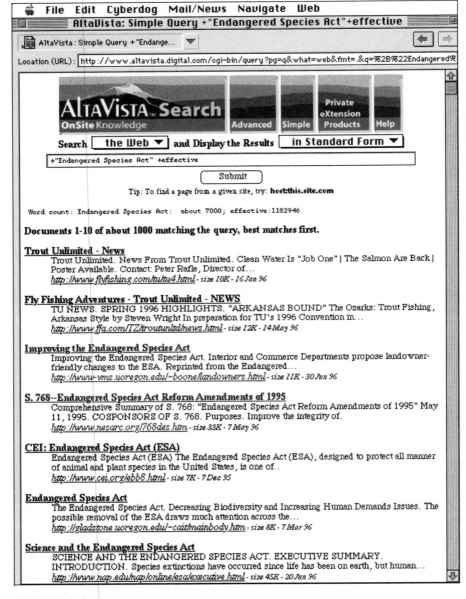

FIGURE 9.1

makes no editorial comments and draws no inferences. It's probably a reliable document.

The second document that looks interesting is entitled *Endangered Species Act*. It is a 1992 report by the Fish and Wildlife Service, an agency of the federal government, which while conceding that "Many land developers, loggers, ranchers and others who rely on the land for revenue would not mind seeing the removal of the ESA altogether. These opponents of the Act claim that it is ineffective, limits growth and simply stands in the way of economically beneficial activities," concludes that the ESA has internal problems, and that far from going too far in its protection of endangered species, often provides help that's too little, too late. Though the document is poorly written and obviously the product of an ESA sympathizer in the FWS, it seems a clear enough analysis of some of the problems in the ESA. Again, a useful document.

Further down the hitlist is an item called *Rep. Smith's Column for February*. It is written by Congressman Nick Smith and is a strong indictment of the ESA, claiming that "our current environmental policies make it harder to save endangered species, impede innovations that can reduce pollution, and waste resources that could be used to improve the quality of our environment" and "in over twenty years, not a single endangered species has ever recovered because of the Act." He concludes "we should repeal the Endangered Species Act and replace it with something that will really work." This article is more problematic, laced with anti-government slogans ("the government is causing a problem") rather than reasons. As a statement of strong emotion, it stands; however, its apparent facts must be taken with a grain of salt because its bias is clear.

Perhaps the most challenging to judge is one entitled *Endangered Species Reform 5/95*. With its impressive name and its glamorous page on the Web, complete with little pictures of the Capitol building in the background, it looks to be an impartial task force charged with gathering and distributing facts. It announces itself as a "Press Release of the Environmental Policy Task Force, a project of The National Center for Public Policy Research." Navigating the site by following one of the links on the page eventually leads to a page called *About the Environmental Policy Task Force*. The first line of the page is "The National Center launched the *Environmental Policy Task Force* to help arm conservatives with tools for the environmental policy debate it had been lacking." With this in mind, it's now possible to use the information and account for the context in which it appears.

Careful reading of the downloaded documents, combined with a memory of recent developments in the area, suggests one more AltaVista search: the controversy over the Spotted Owl in the northwest, a controversy which seemed to focus all the issues and clarify the opposing sides. Using the query +*"spotted owl"* +*"jobs"* uncovers a number of documents on the Web dealing with the jobs versus owls controversy. These are retrieved, and the interesting and especially relevant ones are downloaded for later use as well.

A Gopher search with Veronica turns up the federal site where the complete text of the ESA resides, and a search of CompuServe finds three documents of potential usefulness. An America Online search turns up nothing in this case, as do Archie searches of ftp sites and browsing Yahoo directories to the *Environment and Nature* category. Most listservs who archive their discussions (and not all do) archive them on either gopher- or ftp sites, so it's safe to assume that no archived listservs have dealt with the issue.

The final step of the first-stage search is to search Usenet. Here, DejaNews is the engine of choice. Usenet postings, as mentioned earlier, tend to be wild free-for-alls, with occasional nuggets of real information buried in mountains of passion, name-calling, and charges of ignorance. So a researcher must keep all the weapons of critical analysis at the ready.

A DejaNews Power Search (which allows the construction of more precise queries) using the phrase *Endangered Species Act* (including the quote marks to force a whole phrase search) looks like Figure 9.2. The first twenty-five references DejaNews finds are shown in Figure 9.3.

Many are tangential, however, usually mentioning the phrase *Endangered Species Act* in passing in unrelated contexts or including it in their "sig" (*signature*) file. A few seem appropriate. One in particular, the item listed as *Re: Helen Chenoweth - Super Grunge!,* contains the assertion, "Lastly, the ESA hasn't worked too well. Just 17 species have ever been removed from it . . . 8 due to extinction." Though not providing much support for the ESA overall, it does seem to contradict Representative Smith's assertion (above) that *no* species have been saved by the ESA. Add to this the listing of the duck species whose numbers have increased under the management of the Fish and Wildlife Service (as documented in parts 1 and 2 of the item entitled *Breeding duck number#2/2*) and Rep. Smith is out on a limb, for apparently the ESA has been instrumental in saving some species if we can believe the poster of the *Chenoweth* message and the FWS (source of the *Breeding Duck* message). Whose authority is reliable?

A quick fact-checking trip to the Department of Fish and Wildlife's *Endangered Species Page* (http://www.fws.gov/~r9endspp/endspp.html) uncovers a complete listing of all endangered species and the status of each (a 55-page document!), plus a separate summary table of de-listed species. The summary contains a list of twenty-six species (twenty-three American, three Australian) which have been removed entirely from the

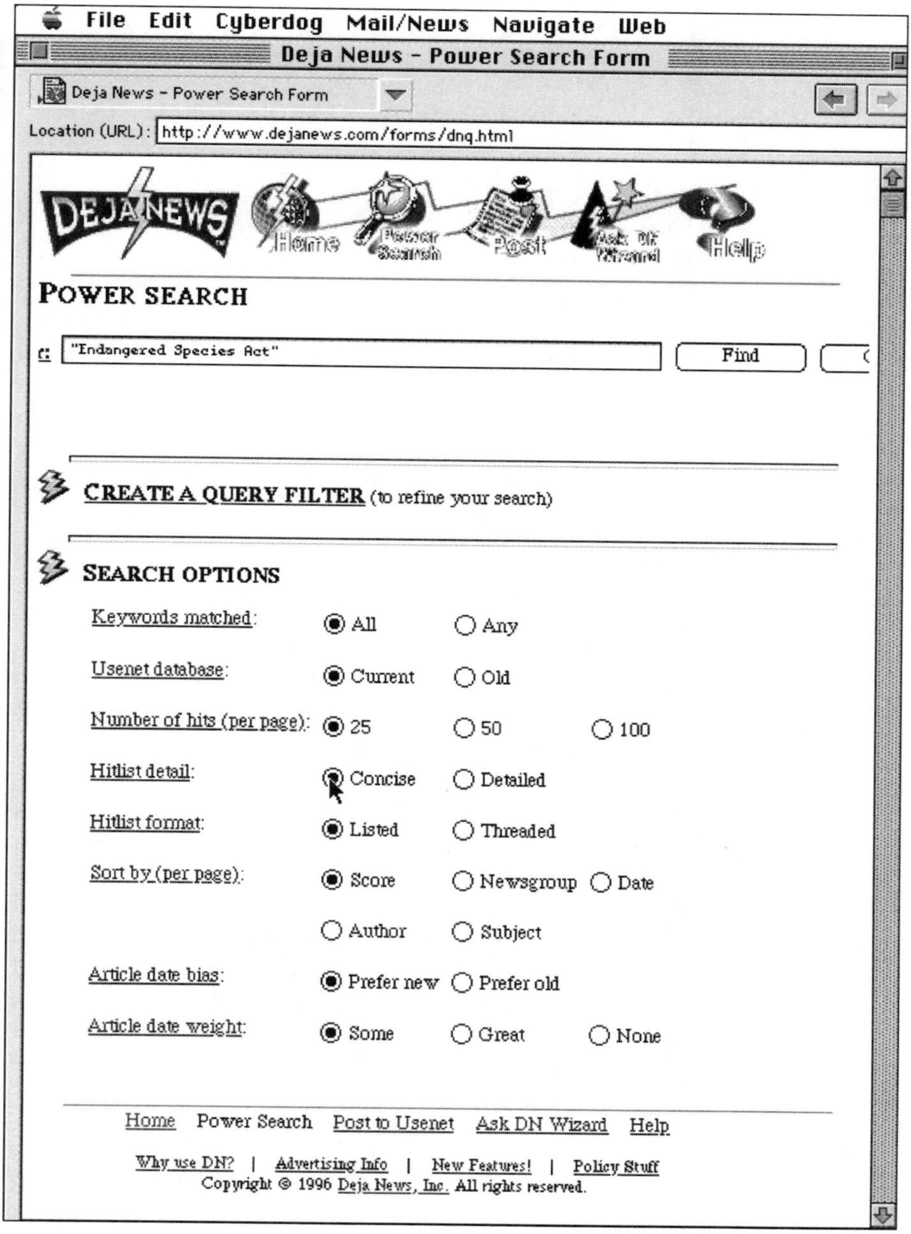
File Edit Cyberdog Mail/News Navigate Web
Deja News - Power Search Form
Deja News - Power Search Form
Location (URL): http://www.dejanews.com/forms/dnq.html
DEJA NEWS
Home
Power Search
Post
Ask DN Wizard
Help
POWER SEARCH
"Endangered Species Act"
Find
CREATE A QUERY FILTER (to refine your search)
SEARCH OPTIONS
Keywords matched: All Any
Usenet database: Current Old
Number of hits (per page): 25 50 100
Hitlist detail: Concise Detailed
Hitlist format: Listed Threaded
Sort by (per page): Score Newsgroup Date
Author Subject
Article date bias: Prefer new Prefer old
Article date weight: Some Great None
Home Power Search Post to Usenet Ask DN Wizard Help
Why use DN? | Advertising Info | New Features! | Policy Stuff
Copyright © 1996 Deja News, Inc. All rights reserved.

FIGURE 9.2

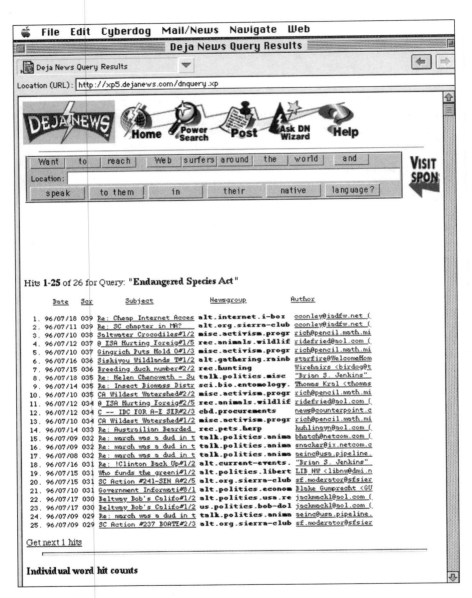

FIGURE 9.3

Endangered Species List. Of the twenty-three, eight are listed as "recovered," that is, no longer in danger of extinction. (All three Australian species are categorized as recovered as well.)

So, armed with all the information gleaned so far from the Internet, here's the final paper, with citations in the MLA format.

FIXING THE ENDANGERED SPECIES ACT

In 1973, Congress enacted the Endangered Species Act, largely in response to the crisis in bald eagle populations. Owing to the widespread use of the pesticide DDT, indiscriminate hunting, and the incursion of civilization into the eagle's natural habitats, the population of the bald eagles had fallen to just four hundred mating pairs, and the species was in critical danger of extinction ("Endangered Species Act: Background"). Sensing that perhaps more species than just the highly visible and politically sensitive bald eagle were in various stages of danger, Congress passed an act to give the federal government far-reaching power to gather data about species and to develop and fund plans for the recovery of species that were identified as endangered. In less than twenty-five years, the bald eagle has been upgraded from endangered to merely threatened (U.S. Fish And Wildlife Service, "Endangered and Threatened"), a significant step in the total recovery of the species. And the Environmental Defense Fund, a pro-conservation group, has concluded, "the truth is that nearly two decades of efforts to preserve the country's most imperiled wildlife have produced results in every state".

Yet, critics of the ESA abound. The heated early-1990s controversy in the northwest lumber regions over the northern spotted owl, a far less appealing object of protection than the national symbol, focused the nation's attention on the ESA. Did it give the federal government too much power, sacrificing human jobs and lives for the sake of a small bird of minimal ecological importance? Did it deny the rights of landowners in its attempts to save the spotted owl? Were people being sacrificed for birds? Furthermore, conservationists and others interested in the preservation of endangered species found the ESA lacking, as well. By the accounts of those who were sympathetic with its aims, the ESA was a dismal failure, providing what one person characterized as merely "emergency room" service (U.S. Fish and Wildlife Service, "Decreasing Biodiversity") for endangered species—too little, too late. From this point of view, the ESA is a

dismal failure. It burdens innocent property owners with mountains of federal red tape and bureaucratic regulations, it restricts
industry so thoroughly that thousands of jobs are lost, and it
doesn't even work. What's the truth about the ESA?

History

As early as 1967 the bald eagle was recognized as being in danger of extinction. Both the spraying of DDT and the hunting of
eagles by ranchers whose herds were being depleted by the preda-
tor had had an enormous effect on the population of the eagle.
Something had to be done to protect the national symbol, and
in 1973 Congress passed the Endangered Species Act. Essentially,
it establishes two categories of at-risk species: endangered and
threatened. An " 'endangered species' is an animal or plant listed
by regulation as being in danger of extinction. A 'threatened
species' is any animal or plant that is likely to become endangered within the foreseeable future" (U.S. Fish and Wildlife Service, "Decreasing Biodiversity"). For both categories, there are
prohibitions against importing into or exporting from the
United States, taking (which includes harassing, harming, pursuing, hunting, shooting, wounding, trapping, killing, captur-
ing, or collecting) within the United States and its territorial seas,
taking on the high seas, possessing, selling, delivering, carrying,
transporting, or shipping any such species unlawfully taken
within the United States or on the high seas, delivering, receiving, carrying, transporting, or shipping in interstate or foreign
commerce in the course of a commercial activity, and selling or
offering for sale in interstate or foreign commerce (Endangered
Species Act). There are penalties assessed for violations and
rewards offered for compliance. Also included is the requirement
to establish and maintain a list of endangered and threatened
species, and the requirement to establish specific plans for the
preservation of each species listed.

The concept of taking has become the most controversial in
recent years, as courts have broadly ruled that taking may
include the disturbing or destruction of an endangered species'
habitat. Thus, cutting down the trees where an endangered
species of bird exists or damming a river where an endangered
fish lives constitutes, under this policy, taking and is therefore
prohibited by law.

The Northern Spotted Owl
and the Logging Industry

Taking as destruction of habitat boiled over in the early 1990s as logging in Washington, Oregon, and northern California was almost entirely halted because the habitat of a rare and endangered species of owl, the northern spotted owl, was being threatened. The spotted owl needs a large expanse of so-called old-growth timber (at least 200 or more years old), and the old growth forests were being rapidly depleted by logging operations. Logging old-growth timber is extremely profitable (a single old-growth tree can be worth $3,000 or more to the logging companies). Thus, the halting of old-growth logging threatened to have major (some feared "devastating") economic effects on the entire northwest U.S. as companies closed, mills shut down, workers lost jobs and either went on welfare or moved out of the area. It seemed as if an entire industry and the region it supported were going to be destroyed—all to save a small owl.

Complicating the issue has been the spotted owl's designation as an indicator species, which means it has been found to be a general indicator of the overall health of an entire ecosystem. This means that if the spotted owl is endangered, then so is the entire ecosystem that it inhabits.

Emotions ran high as the logging industry and others (particularly property-rights organizations such as America First) squared off against the environmentalists, with angry charges and counter-charges being made. Then-President Bush, campaigning for re-election in 1992, told a gathering of lumberworkers, "We'll be up to our necks in owls and every millworker will be out of a job" (qtd. Wallace). The environmentalists countered with, "industry groups succeeded in creating a 'jobs vs. the owl' mentality all across America," and characterized the loggers' complaints as a "disinformation campaign," adding "large timber companies have used the spotted owl imbroglio to raise prices and increase market share" (Craven).

The campaigns reached full force in 1995, as the ESA was up for renewal and the Republican majority in Congress tried to cut funding for the act. At roughly the same time, the court case *Bruce Babbitt v. Sweet Home Chapter of Communities for a Great Oregon* reaffirmed the interpretation of taking as alteration of habitat, effectively shutting down much logging in the Northwest and further angering opponents of the ESA. To reverse some of the effects of the Sweet Home decision, Congress passed the controversial Salvage Logging bill, which explicitly allows for certain kinds of logging to be re-instituted.

The ESA: Has It Worked?

Criticism of the ESA falls into three basic categories: It's ineffective, it stands in the way of economic development, and it violates the rights of private property owners. Congressman Nick Smith has claimed, "In fact, in over twenty years, not a single endangered species has ever recovered because of the Act" (Smith). Even scientists charged with evaluating the effectiveness of the Act have concluded "Changes are needed in the way biological populations and habitat are designated for protection under the Endangered Species Act," noting that in many cases the Act works, but in some cases the panel "recommend[s] changes to improve its effectiveness" (National Research Council). Smith's is an extreme view, for while a number of factors may have contributed to the restoration of the bald eagle, for example, few would deny that the Endangered Species Act was central to saving the national symbol. Though there are different ways of measuring success, by any measurement the ESA has saved some species from extinction. Writes Julia Bumbaca of the U.S. Fish and Wildlife Service, "To date [January, 1995], eight species have been recovered and removed from the endangered species list, but more than 25 are approaching recovery goals and may be reclassified from endangered to threatened, or delisted in the near future. Some 38 percent of all species now on the list are either stable or improving, critically important steps on the road to recovery." Another count puts the number higher, but without supporting evidence: "The act has proven successful restoring the numbers of over 46 species that may have vanished without protection" (Torres). Couple the small numbers of species saved with the economic and lifestyle damage done to mill workers, sheep farmers, and general property-owners, and one has to ask: "Has it been worth it?"

On the Other Hand

The "jobs versus owls" conflict, it appears, was so much smoke and mirrors by the timber industry. While the logging industry was actively stirring up fears about job losses due to the spotted owl, in actuality "six years after the northern spotted owl raised the specter of massive job losses in the Pacific Northwest, the fear of Appalachian poverty is more phobia than fact," concluded Peter Sleeth, a reporter for the Oregonian. Sleeth discovered "In the past six years, 16,695 direct wood products jobs were lost in Oregon, Washington, and Idaho. That's far below the 65,700 direct jobs predicted to be lost by the Northwest Forest Resource Council in 1989, based solely on reduced timber harvests in Western Oregon and Washington. It's even below the government forecasts of at least 20,000 lost jobs."

Furthermore, "In the boardrooms of the 12 largest publicly traded timber and lumber companies, all is smug: For these companies, profits were up 43 percent in 1994 compared to 1993. According to an industry newsletter, prices almost doubled between 1990 and 1994" (Craven). And, overall, "Between 1989 and 1994, Oregon lost 15,000 forest-related jobs. But during the same period the state gained 20,000 jobs in other areas such as high technology" (Craven). While complaining loudly and publicly about losses, the timber industry was making enormous profits. States like Oregon were converting their economies to be less timber-based and actually showed a net gain of jobs during the height of the industry-induced terror about lost jobs.

There were jobs lost, and every one of those lost jobs has a personal, a family, and a social tragedy associated with it. But you never really hear about the individuals who lost their jobs and their livelihoods—all you ever hear about is the how the timber industry is suffering. And as an industry, it's clearly not suffering.

More to the point, then, are the two remaining questions: does the ESA allow the government too much power at the expense of individual property owners, and is the ESA effective?

It does appear, however, that the provisions that allow the federal government to take over, without compensation, management of land where endangered species live is both unethical and probably unconstitutional. Writes Nancie Marzulla, "The Court's decision in *Sweet Home* provides the government with a 'blank check' with which it can destroy an individual's entire investment in land or private enterprise." Furthermore, the Fifth Amendment to the Constitution states, in part, ". . . nor shall private property be taken for public use without just compensation." Yet the ESA gives exactly that power to the federal government in the name of species protection. Even though the "individuals" crying the most loudly over loss of private property are the logging companies, small landowners and even individual homeowners are being punished unfairly. There is currently no relief for the homeowner who finds an endangered species on his land.

Even more troublesome is the apparent ineffectiveness of the Act in recovering the very species it's designed to protect. Despite some well-publicized success stories such as the bald eagle, only eight species have been fully recovered out of roughly 600 native species listed ("Endangered Species Act: Background") as endangered—not a high success rate. And even if we grant the ESA Fact Sheets' claim of 25 "approaching recovery goals" and "38 percent of all species now on the list are either stable or improving" (Bumbaca) (stable and improving are, by the way, not recognized categories in the ESA, and there is no agreed-upon method of defining such terms precisely), the best possible scenario is that 62 percent of the time, the ESA is failing in its ultimate goal. In fact, a report by the Fish and Wildlife Service confirms this very conclusion: "The 1992 report, under the action of the ESA, shows a jump from 11 to 14 extinct species and 219 to 232 species declining. This data does not read well for the ESA . . ." (U.S. Fish and Wildlife Service, "Decreasing Biodiversity"). According to a panel of the National Academy of Science established by Congress to review the Act, "The ultimate goal of the Endangered Species Act is to ensure the long-term survival of a species, but the recovery plans designed to achieve this goal often are developed too slowly or have provisions that cannot be justified scientifically" (National Research Council). These recommended changes include quicker identification of endangered species and the quick establishment of more aggressive and coherent recovery plans for each species listed as endangered.

Recently, Secretary of the Interior Bruce Babbitt and James Baker, Undersecretary of Commerce, released *Ten principles to improve ESA implementation,* a statement outlining their view of needed adjustments in the Act and its implementation. Of the ten, four ("Treat landowner fairly and with consideration," "Minimize social and economic impacts," "Create incentives for landowners to conserve species," and "Provide quick, responsive answers and certainty to landowners") directly address the issue of individual property rights. The remaining six are designed to speed up the workings of the Act and to streamline its implementation with both earlier intervention to prevent future endangered species and to hurry along the recovery programs currently in place for species already endangered ("Improving the Endangered Species Act").

These principles, not yet official policies, seem rational and promising. They will work to preserve endangered species as vigorously as possible, while still protecting the rights of private property owners. Implementing them will be complex and difficult, granted, but they represent the best solution we have so far.

Works Cited

Bumbaca, Julia. "Endangered Species Fact Sheets." ESFACTS.TXT, CompuServe Information Service, Animals Forum, Endangered Species Library (28 July 1996).

Craven, Bill. "Spotted Owls and the Attorney General." http://falcon.cc.ukans.edu/~tshistar/pa081195.html. (26 July 1996).

"Endangered Species Act." http://ash.lab.r1.fws.gov/cargo/es.html (23 July 1996).

"Endangered Species Act: Background." http://nceet.snre.umich.edu/Curriculum/esa.html. (15 July 1996).

Environmental Defense Fund. "A Record of Endangered Species Act Successes." http://www.edf.org/pubs/EDF-Letter/1993/Jan/d_endspe.html (19 July 1996).

"Improving the Endangered Species Act." http://www-vms.uoregon.edu/~boone/landowners.html. (22 July 1996).

Marzulla, Nancie G. "Are Property Rights Facing Extinction?" http://www.offroad.com/green/espa_abuse.html. (12 August 1996).

National Research Council. "Science Panel Recommends Changes." gopher://xerxes.nas.edu:70/00/onpi/pr/esa/esa.txt (11 July 1996).

Smith, Nick. "Column by Congressman Nick Smith for the Week of February 25, 1996." http://www.house.gov/nicksmith/columns/col6225.htm (26 July 1996).

Torres, Chris J. "Endangering the Endangered Species Act." http://naio.kcc.hawaii.edu/bosp/Kapio/OCT_10_95/Endangeredspecies.html (22 July 1996).

U.S. Fish And Wildlife Service. "Endangered and Threatened Wildlife and Plants; Final Rule to Reclassify the Bald Eagle From Endangered to Threatened in All of the Lower 48 States." http://www.fws.gov/~r9endspp/fr95580.html (21 August 1996).

———. "The Endangered Species Act: Decreasing Biodiversity and Increasing Human Demands Issues." http://gladstone.uoregon.edu/~cait/mainbody.htm (24 July 1996).

Wallace, Richard L. "Why Endangered Species Protection vs. Economic Development Doesn't Have to Be a Win–Lose Scenario." http://www.spectacle.org/196/rich1.html (25 July 1996).

Appendix 1

A CRITICAL LOOK
AT A USENET THREAD

The following is an actual exchange that took place over the period of
June 19, 1996 to July 5, 1996, on the Usenet group alt.folklore.science.
The postings are real; the names and other identifying material have
been changed or deleted to preserve the anonymity of the posters. Individual contributors are referred to as "Poster #." In addition, no corrections of spelling, grammatical, or typing mistakes have been made.

This thread is very typical of Usenet. The one exception is that the discussion remains civil and courteous, for the most part. There's no name-
calling, no flaming, but there is genuine disagreement and attempts to
prove a particular point of view.

For readability, the text of the postings themselves will be in Courier
typeface, `like this`. The few header lines reproduced for each message
will be in boldface, **like this.** Notes, comments, discussion, and interpretations will be interspersed between postings in italics, *like this.*

Subject: Electric cars: Less pollution?
From: Poster 1
Date: 1996/06/19

```
Electric cars supposedly create less pollution than
their gas-guzzling cousins. However, putting batteries
in cars just means that their ultimate energy source is
the electrical power plant across town. Suppose a bat-
tery stores 50% of the energy put into it (which is
wildly optimistic). Then that power plant would have to
```

generate twice as much energy for a given amount of driving than would a conventional car.

On the other hand, electrical plants have the capability of "scrubbing" their emissions--they may emit more in total than cars but emit far less on a watt for watt basis.

Who knows the answer: which the lesser pollutant, electric or gasoline?

Poster 1, Biomedical Physicist (Anesthesiology)
    U of MD Medical Systems and Medical School
    R Adams Cowley Shock Trauma Center
    Baltimore, Maryland 21201

Here's the opening observation/question for this thread. The poster has thrown out a comment for the reaction of the other readers of the group. It's mildly provocative, and the poster may reasonably expect some kind of answer, but there's no way of knowing, on June 16, how much if any response will be elicited.

Subject: Re: Electric cars: Less pollution?
From: Poster 2
Date: 1996/06/20

Hydro-electric power (the *only* reasonable power source here) has 0% emissions. Beat that on a watt for watt basis!

This poster has a brief answer, but he doesn't really answer the question posed by poster 1. But, interestingly, watch how most of the succeeding posters actually reply to this post rather than the initial one. There's controversy brewing, with this poster's seeming announcement that hydro-electric power is the only reasonable power source.

Subject: Re: Electric cars: Less pollution?
From: Poster 3
Date: 1996/06/20

Poster 1 is right, it's easiest to treat one big problem than a billion little ones. i think you've thrown in a

red-herring with the hydro-electricity option. i guess
you could of thrown in a salmon--but i don't think there
are any left!!! dam!

*This poster agrees with poster 1, but he merely asserts a reason—"it's easiest
to treat one big problem . . ." Is this necessarily so?*

Subject: Re: Electric cars: Less pollution?
From: Poster 4
Date: 1996/06/20

Er, not quite. After the flooding of a valley to produce a hydroelectric reservoir, residual vegetation on
the valley floor decomposes anaerobically over a long
period, releasing large amounts of various gases--
including methane, carbon dioxide and sulphurous
oxides--into the atmosphere.

In some cases, the volume of harmful gases produced
over the working life of a dam can approach that of a
comparable fossil fuel power station over the same
period. The problem seems to be particularly bad in
Brazil, which has a huge hydroelectric programme, and
similarly huge expanses of dense rainforest vegetation.

This hidden source of pollution was the subject of an
article in a recent issue of New Scientist magazine,
and Canada was mentioned because of its extensive
hydropower schemes; indeed, I seem to remember that
most of the studies described were Canadian. I'll dig
out some more details if anyone is interested.

*A fourth poster enters the discussion, and note how reasonable, how knowl-
edgeable, he seems. And again, he's responding to the second poster, not the
original one. He's tactful as he begins his disagreement ("Er, not quite . . .")
and he brings up a new point that no one has mentioned, or apparently even
thought of. This is typical of open-ended Usenet discussions—new ideas and
knowledge are always being thrown into the mix. This person is believable—
he sounds like he knows what he's talking about.*

Subject: Re: Electric cars: Less pollution?
From: Poster 4
Date: 1996/06/25

Some people sent me emails about this, and after much
scrabbling around, I found the article--New Scientist
No 2028, 4 May 1996, pp. 28-31 "Trouble bubbles for
hydropower".

Below is an extract from the article, disussing the
Balbina dam, on the River Uatuma, a tributary of the
Amazon in Brazil.

---Snip---

"At Balbina, [Philip] Fearnside has aggregated the
greenhouse effect of methane and CO_2 (*) to give a 'CO2
equivalent', that he can compare directly with emissions from fossil-fuel power stations. He calculates
that Balbina emitted the equivalent of more than 12
million tonnes of CO_2 in its first year [1988]. That
figure fell to some 7 million tonnes in 1990 and to
around 2 million tonnes last year. It will slip below 1
million tonnes in about 10 years' time, and drop to 0.5
million tonnes in perhaps 50 years.

"How do these figures compare with conventional power
stations? Balbina's average output of electricity in
the first eight years of its operation was 112
megawatts--not much for a reservoir the size of an English county. It floods the equivalent of two soccer
pitches to generate enough power to run a 1-kilowatt
electric fire.

"If the Balbina dam had not been built, the authorities
in Manaus would probably have constructed a conventional power station burning diesel and fuel oil. Such
a plant would have produced annual emissions--almost
all of it carbon dioxide - of some 0.4 million tonnes,
says Fearnside. So far, Balbina has had something like
16 times as potent a greenhouse effect as an equivalent
fossil-fuel power station. And, says Fearnside, it will

continue to be more polluting 'for 50 years, and probably indefinitely'."

---Snip---

*--this 'CO2 equivalence' assigns methane a greenhouse
effect 11 times as potent as CO2 (whether this is by
mass or by volume is not made clear in the article).
The factor used in different studies varies widely--in
a Canadian Freshwater Research Institute study of 1993,
the factor used was 60. Based on the Canadian studies,
it is estimated that hydropower produces 400 million
tonnes of 'CO2 equivalent' annually, or 7 per cent of
total man-made emissions of CO2. Even erring on the
conservative side, and following Fearnside's estimate,
the polluting effect of hydropower would seem to be far
from negligible, especially when you consider that
hydropower is still very much a minority energy source.

Apparently, this poster, still poster 4, has received personal email (a very common—and commendable—practice. Don't clutter up the on-line discussion with material meant only for one person!). But his reply pertains to the topic of the thread and is appropriate for all readers, so he posts it to the group. It's a long post, taken from a respectable scientific magazine, that presents the findings of research to back up his earlier point about the gases from hydroelectric power.

Subject: Re: Electric cars: Less pollution?
From: Poster 5
Date: 1996/06/20

Obviously you can't. But you need to also concede that
hydroelectric power cannot supply all of the electricity needed and acknowledge that most areas don't have
the resources needed for hydroelectric power (you need
a big waterfall or very fast river . . .)

Poster 5 is responding to poster 2's final challenge—"beat that. . . ." And he, too, adds new insights. Not new information, as poster 4 did, but he still forces poster 2 to rethink his position by bringing up something else no one has thought of.

Subject: Re: Electric cars: Less pollution?
From: Poster 6
Date: 1996/06/20

I agree it's a good power source--but let's not get
carried away. Hydropower has enviromental impact too.
As an example, look at the Glen Canyon dam. They
recently tried to "simulate" a spring flood with it,
partially to restore sandbar formation on the Grand
Canyon. And most of the fish species in the Canyon have
been eliminated or greatly reduced by the temperature
change (ie--the river gets much colder because you're
releasing water through the bottom. Another point--the
Colorado no longer even reaches the ocean due to human
use. Yes, this has to do with hydroelectric--at least
part of that water is lost due to evaporation from
reservoirs (lakes behind dams).

It *is* a good power source--but I don't want to loose
any more wild rivers or beautiful canyons for it. I
just have a problem with you saying it's the *only*
reasonable source (not true IMHO), and say it has 0%
emissions (true) as if that was the only goal.

*Poster 6 has replied also to poster 2, particularly his assertion about the rea-
sonableness of hydroelectric power. Also, he has replied before poster 4's rejoin-
ders about the emissions of dam sites has arrived at the newsgroup. Sometimes
it can be a matter of hours for a message to actually reach the group. He brings
up another issue—the destruction of wilderness and animal habitats, to further refute poster 2's position.*

Subject: Re: Electric cars: Less pollution?
From: Poster 2
Date: 1996/06/21

I agree with your intent. But if you look closely, i
said it's the only reasonable power source ->here<-,
which means "where i live". In fact, hydro power is
probably the single largest employer of electrical
engineers in my province. We have an overabundance of
lakes and rivers, but not much else to generate power.
(except the wind at portage & main)

>I agree it's a good power source--but let's not
>get carried away. Hydropower has enviromental
>impact too. As an example, look at the Glen

Yes. A few months ago i visited the Hoover Dam (which
is about 1/2 an hour from vegas--those 'gears: they go
to vegas, but want to see some silly dam), and was
devastated by the amount of territory that was now
under water because of it. (Lake Mead)

The north of our province is where our Hydro-power generating stations are. 99/100 of the population is *not*
there, so we don't get very many people caring about
the environment that gets flooded, especially since it
is borderline tundra. It provides all of the power for
Manitoba, parts of Ontario, and parts of the Northern
U.S. A. I really don't know how much of an environmental impact it has had. In terms of emissions to the
environment, though, it is borderline nil. (some from
the machines used to build the dams).

Poster 2 finally jumps back in to defend himself. He corrects the misreadings of the previous posters (they misinterpreted his intentions, a common occurrence in newsgroups, and so in the ebb and flow of the discussion, mistakes get corrected, misunderstandings are set right, and problems get solved). In addition, he adds some factual information to the discussion, and admits when he's unsure about something. He seems believable.

Subject: Re: Electric cars: Less pollution?
From: Poster 7
Date: 1996/06/20

In article <4qahbg$60f@vixen.cso.uiuc.edu>
   Poster 5 writes:

>most areas don't have the resources needed for
>hydroelectric power (you need a big waterfall or
>very fast river . . .)

>

No. No. No. Waterfalls are horribly lossy and the
velocity of a river is no indication of the energy

available. A squirt from a water pistol may have plenty of velocity but not much energy. Hydroelectric power depends on water volume and potential difference as a result of the source water's height above sealevel.

The Norwegians are cunning buggers. They find a lake in the mountains, sitting quietly and harming no one but pregnant with potential energy, and surreptitiously bore a horizontal hole into the side of the mountains, well beneath the lake. Once they're under the centre of the lake, they start boring upwards . . . It's a some-what hazardous process but the end result is a huge whoosh of water. The survivors quickly jam a turbine in the hole which provides other Norwegians with oodles of electricity. All done without rivers or waterfalls. This technique does explain why Norway doesn't have many Norwegians and why the turtles never complain about the weight of the Norwegian population.

This is a tough one to read—there's the strange word "lossy" (a typo? A nonce-word?). There's the very convincing analogy with the water-pistol which refutes the previous poster's assertion about the velocity needed from a waterfall for energy in real, understandable terms. Then there's the reasonable explanation, seemingly valid scientifically, about volume and potential difference. More grist for this thread's mill. Then there's the bizarre story about drilling holes in the sides of mountains. Is this true? Is this tongue in cheek? (Most Usenet veterans have given up trying to be subtly ironic or sarcastic—irony apparently doesn't carry well without facial expressions to accompany it. Most irony gets misunderstood in the Internet.)

Subject: Re: Electric cars: Less pollution?
From: Poster 8
Date: 1996/06/24

Poster 7 wrote:

: In article <4qahbg$60f@vixen.cso.uiuc.edu>
: Poster 5 writes:
:
: >most areas don't have the resources needed for
: >hydroelectric power (you need a big waterfall or
: >very fast river . . .)
: >

: No. No. No. Waterfalls are horribly lossy and the
: velocity of a river is no indication of the energy
: available. A squirt from a water pistol may have
: plenty of velocity but not much energy. Hydroelectric
: power depends on water volume and potential
: difference as a result of the source water's
: height above sealevel.

Unless you do what is common in these parts . . . Just
run a vertical pipe next to the water fall and take
advantage of the water pressure in the manner normally
associated with hydroelectric damns. Yeah, you don't
get the flood control advantages associated with a
damn, but then, the whole mess is one hell of a lot
cheaper.

This posting needs a good deal of clarification. It's not clear exactly what the poster is referring to. If you were going to use this information in your own writing, you'd have to either wait for someone to ask poster 8 to clarify this, or you'd have to do it yourself (probably off-group, in a personal email correspondence).

Subject: Re: Electric cars: Less pollution?
From: Poster 9
Date: 1996/06/21

In article <4qahbg$60f@vixen.cso.uiuc.edu>,
Poster 5 wrote:

>Poster 2 writes:

>

>>In article <4q90f0$2abp@trout.ab.umd.edu>,
>>Poster 1 wrote:
>>>
>>>On the other hand, electrical plants have the
>>>capability of "scrubbing" their emissions--they may
>>>emit more in total than cars but emit far less on a
>>>watt for watt basis.

>

>>Hydro-electric power (the *only* reasonable power
>>source here) has 0% emissions. Beat that on a watt
>>for watt basis!

>Obviously you can't. But you need to also concede
>that hydroelectric power cannot supply all of the
>electricity needed and acknowledge that most areas
>don't have the resources needed for hydroelectric
>power (you need a big waterfall or very fast
>river . . .)

You also have to be willing to drown a lot of land,
which must itself must cost a lot. And you must eventually reckon with the inevitability of silting, which
will ultimately render any dam more or less useless and
destroy any flood control advantage conferred by the
then non-existent reservoir. About the only truly harm-
less place for hydroelectricity is at a waterfall or
rapids with a high head and a large natural reservoir,
such as at Niagara Falls.

Of particular concern should be the loss of reservoir
capacity. Downstream of Hoover Dam the old flood plain
has been developed by towns and resorts, which have
depended on the elimination of the one-time huge floods
on the Colorado River. The loss of flood control capacity now represents a huge future financial loss. Even
the occasional controlled releases at Hoover Dam have
caused some flooding along the lower river.

Perhaps this cannot be made a part of a pollution com-
parison, but it is not so clear that hydro constitutes
a true advantage over some of the more polluting modes
of generating power.

The mini-tsunami at an Italian hydro facility a decade
or so ago is an example of another of the dangers
inherent in hydroelectricity. In that case, a landslide
along the steep sides of the reservoir's valley caused
a large wave which overtopped the dam and caused con-
siderable destruction downstream along with loss of
life.

Should the anticipated earthquake occur at the location
of the new hydro installation in India's Himalayan
foothills, we may see an even more cataclysmic result
of hydropower.

The first thing to notice about this posting is the quote-within-a-quote-within-a-quote. Poster 9 has here quoted poster 5, who quoted poster 2, who quoted poster 1. This is normally good procedure for keeping your readers straight, but in this case it's overkill, and makes for difficult reading. Again, however, the poster seems knowledgeable in his references to actual facts and events and his detailed understand of yet a new set of problems associated with hydroelectric power. It's the detail that gives this poster the sense of authoritativeness we feel. If need be, we could find out more about his references to India and the Hoover Dam—directly from him, if necessary. There's reliable information here, it seems.

Subject: Re: Electric cars: Less pollution?
From: Poster 10
Date: 1996/06/19

In article <4q90f0$2abp@trout.ab.umd.edu>,
Poster 1 wrote:

[. . .]

>Who knows the answer: which the lesser pollutant,
>electric or gasoline?

I think the answer is "it depends". I've seen calculations showing it both ways. If you assume that the
utility has to burn coal or gas to make the power for
the recharging and that the energy used by the car is
constant, the gasoline car seems to win. If hydroelectric generation is used the electric car wins.

The real crunch comes when the batteries have to be
replaced. If the batteries are lead acid it is a night-
mare. At present the recycling of lead acid batteries
it a very dirt process and often done in third world
counties.

Here at last we have someone attempting to answer Poster 1. Note that the "Subject" line of the postings has stayed the same: Electric cars: Less pollution? Yet, the actual discussion has drifted very quickly to the merits of hydroelectric power—absolutely unpredictably. This poster notes that he's "seen calculations" but he doesn't provide the group with them. A follow-up question is in order here, if you were going to use this poster's ideas. And he introduces another negative point about batteries—disposing of them.

Subject: Re: Electric cars: Less pollution?
From: Poster 11
Date: 1996/06/27

Poster 1 wrote:

```
: Electric cars supposedly create less pollution than
: their gas-guzzling cousins. However, putting
: batteries in cars just means that their ultimate
: energy source is the electrical power plant across
: town. Suppose a battery stores 50% of the energy put
: into it (which is wildly optimistic). Then that power
: plant would have to generate twice as much energy for
: a given amount of driving than would a conventional
: car.

: On the other hand, electrical plants have the
: capability of "scrubbing" their emissions--they may
: emit more in total than cars but emit far less on a
: watt for watt basis.

: Who knows the answer: which the lesser pollutant,
: electric or gasoline?
```

Nobody yet!

But there are alternative ways of generating electricity under development around the world which could be much cleaner than present methods.

And also as you point out, generating plants would have the pollution source of however many cars all in one place. I think at present the idea of getting the pollution 'off the streets' is a good start--at least we may be able to reduce the alarming escalation in asthma sufferers, esp. children, and address the problem of global pollution at a greatly reduced number of sources, which I think would be more practical.

The debate continues . . .

Another response to the first poster. He asserts there are cleaner alternative ways of producing power, but, as we've seen in the tangential debate on hydro-electric power, which was initially claimed to be a reasonable alternative, this assertion is fraught with difficulties. Be skeptical of this one. Perhaps a follow-up question is in order here. There are also some logic problems here (why is getting pollution off the street a good start—why does it matter where the pollution's source is?), and some really shaky assumptions about the relationship of pollution and asthma. There are some ideas here, but little substance. Mostly opinion.

Subject: Re: Electric cars: Less pollution?
From: Poster 12
Date: 1996/06/28

Also keep in mind that while an automobile engine is run at wildly varying speed-load combinations, an electric generation facility probably runs its source (whatever it may be) at the most efficient condition. Or at least it tries to.

This factor may help even out the efficiency loss from batteries stated earlier.

The same concept is considered for hybrid electric vehicles. Have batteries and motor supplimented by a small engine (or gas turbine in the example that I'm thinking of) which turns a generator. The auxiliary power source always runs at the most efficient conditions.

Poster 12
Department of Metallurgical and Materials Engineering
Colorado School of Mines

This poster seems to be associated with an engineering school, so (unless he's fabricating that, which doesn't seem likely) he has some initial authority. He brings up another point—the efficiency (or lack of it) of automobile engines, and suggests a possible implication for the issue at hand. He seems knowl-edgeable, and seems to have some more valuable insights.

Subject: Hydro Energy (was Re: Electric cars: Less pol-
**   lution?)**
From: Poster 2
Date: 1996/06/30

Hi, i'm the guy that made the comment before about
hydro generated energy being the only reasonable way to
generate power, but most of you that replied missed the
last word, which was "here". I should have been more
explicit, but by "here", i meant Southern Manitoba,
Canada. Yes, there are bad points to it, like flooding
of land. In my case, the power is actually generated in
near-tundra land way way up north. I do not have
details, and i'm sure it still disrupts some natural
habitats, but it likely doesn't disturb too much in
tundra, as opposed to the U.S. hydro generating, which
floods out habitats, arable land, and adds to visual
pollution. Please correct me if i am wrong about the
habitats up north.

When compared to the vast amounts of cheap energy we
can produce, no other form of electrical power generation makes sense here. (except maybe harnessing the
wind from all the politicians) I look forward to the
day when we all have solar panels on our homes that
are also linked into the power grid. Until that
day . . . all you people in the Northern US keep buying
power from us. :-)

*Poster 2 returns again to clarify and defend his original posting. Of interest is
the fact that he has changed the subject line for the thread. The thread long ago
took leave of its original topic (electric cars), but most posters continued to use
the same subject (which is filled in automatically by most email and newsreader programs, making it the path of least resistance). He tries to create a
common ground of agreement ("yes, there are bad points to it. . . .") but he jus-
tifies hydro power in his own context, and reasserts that he actually did say
"here." And he admits the points where he doesn't have all the facts. This is a
rational, reasonable, persuasive post, and it points the direction where a follow-
up is needed (the tundra issue, which could be researched further).*

Subject: **Re: Hydro Energy (was Re: Electric cars: Less pollution?)**
From: **Poster 13**
Date: **1996/07/01**

Poster 2 wrote:

: Hi, i'm the guy that made the comment before about
: hydro generated energy being the only reasonable way
: to generate power, but most of you that replied
: missed the last word, which was "here". I should have
: been more explicit, but by "here", i meant Southern
: Manitoba, Canada. Yes, there are bad points to it,
: like flooding of land. In my case, the power is
: actually generated in near-tundra land way way up
: north. I do not have details, and i'm sure it still
: disrupts some natural habitats, but it likely doesn't
: disturb too much in tundra, as opposed to the U.S.
: hydro generating, which floods out habitats, arable
: land, and adds to visual pollution. Please correct
: me if i am wrong about the habitats up north.

: When compared to the vast amounts of cheap energy we
: can produce, no other form of electrical power
: generation makes sense here. (except maybe harnessing
: the wind from all the politicians) I look forward to
: the day when we all have solar panels on our homes
: that are also linked into the power grid. Until that
: day . . . all you people in the Northern US keep
: buying power from us. :-)

What about nuclear? Why doesn't anybody bring up
nuclear power? It has extremely low emissions compared
to fossil fuel burning plants (and as some posters have
suggested compared to hydroelectric as well). Besides,
what better place than northern canada is there for a
long-term storage facility for nuclear waste?

*As you might imagine, the discussion now leaves the topics of electric cars and
hydroelectric power completely, as the remaining eight posts to this thread pick
up the theme of nuclear energy, and the discussion is diverted entirely. Not a
bad thing, necessarily, and in fact it's pretty common on Usenet. But since this*

much of the thread will suffice for the purposes of comment and analysis, we can safely leave the discussion of nuclear power.

THE RESULTS

It's fascinating to watch the meanderings of thought and idea and information during a thread. Each statement that seems definitive and convincing is usually modified, added to, or sometimes even contradicted entirely. The end result is usually a good discussion, with lots of information and interpretations to pick from and synthesize for yourself.

Seldom is there a real sense of closure, however. Most discussions just fizzle out as readers grow tired and lose interest or the thread itself is exhausted. In many cases, a new thread is born out of something said in the old thread, and the newsgroup chugs along.

What has happened in this particular thread? What is useful here, if you're writing a research paper on, say, hydroelectric power?

1. You've seen that not only are there two sides to an issue, there are at least half a dozen, all laid out for you in moderate detail here.
2. There is good information here: the floods from Hoover dam, the gases emitted by flooded damsites, the difficulty of disposing of used batteries, the fundamental principles of physics that apply to energy production by dams, and so on. This material may be quoted confidently, and, if need be, it can be further verified.
3. There's some foolishness here: irony (apparently) that doesn't work, assertions that may or may not be true (but certainly have no evidence to support them), misinterpretations of posters' words.
4. There are authorities here. Some of the posters have real credentials; some earn the right to be listened to by their insight and knowledge and careful interpretation of facts. When they don't know something, they say so, and let someone else fill in the gaps.
5. There's no conclusion. That's for you, the reader/writer, to fill in. You have the facts; you've seen the issues; you've seen the arguments made and refuted; your eyes are open.

Appendix **2**

DOCUMENTING SOURCES FROM THE INTERNET

In general, the rules for documenting Internet sources are the same as for other sources: both MLA and APA use the in-text citation method. But there are some differences between on-line sources and print sources—lack of page numbers and lack of publication date, to name two examples. And information on the Net is subject to change—material is rewritten, moved, removed, duplicated, linked to. So, especially in the eyes of the MLA, it's important to note *when* you accessed a certain site. In the discussion that follows, only the special instances of citing on-line sources will be handled. For a complete guide to academic (print and other traditional sources) citation, use a good writing handbook or consult the MLA or APA guides directly.

MLA STYLE

This set of additions to the *MLA Handbook for Writers of Research Papers* was first designed by Janice Walker (http://www.cas.usf.edu/english/walker/mla.html), and later incorporated into the *MLA Handbook,* 4th edition. In general, it applies the principles used by MLA to the special cases of on-line sources. Note that in-text citations remain the same as with regular print sources, that is, author's last name in parentheses following the cited material.

WWW Sites (World Wide Web)

Author's name, the full title of the work in quotation marks, the title of the complete work if applicable in italics, the full URL, and the date of visit.

U.S. Fish and Wildlife Service. "Program Overview." *Endangered Species Home Page.* http://www.fws.gov/~r9endspp/programs.html (15 July 1996).

FTP Sites

Author's name (reversed), the title (which is not necessarily the same as the filename) of the paper (in quotation marks), and the full URL of the paper, that is, the address of the ftp site along with the full path to follow to find the file, and the date of access.

Deutsch, Peter. "archie—An Electronic Directory Service for the Internet." ftp://ftp.sura.net/pub/archie/docs/whatis.archie (15 July 1996).

Gopher Sites

Author's name, the title of the paper in quotation marks, any print publication information, the Gopher URL, and the date of access.

Massachusetts Higher Education Coordinating Council. "Using Coordination And Collaboration To Address Change." gopher://gopher.mass.edu:170/00gopher_root%3A%5B_hecc%5D_plan (15 July 1996).

Telnet Sites

Author's name (if applicable), the title of the work in quotation marks, the title of the full work if applicable in italics, the complete URL, and the date of visit. Include other additional directions to access the particular file as necessary.

"Hubble Space Telescope Daily Report #1712." STINFO Bulletin Board (9 June 1996). telnet stinfo.hq.eso.org; login as "stinfo" (21 Sept. 1996).

Email, Listserv, and Usenet Citations

Author's name (if known), the subject in quotation marks, the address of the listserv or newsgroup, and the date of the posting.

Liberty Northwest. "Who funds the greenies." alt.politics.libertarian (15 July 1996).

Schultz, Joan. "Re: Halley's Comet." Personal email (15 Jan. 1996)

MOOs, MUDs, IRC, etc.

The name of the speaker(s) and type of communication (i.e., Personal Interview or MOO posting), the address if applicable, and the date in parentheses.

> Guest. Personal Interview. telnet du.edu 8888 (18 August 1996).

APA STYLE

The *Publication Manual of the American Psychological Association* (4th ed.) is fairly dated in its handling of on-line sources, having been published before the rise of the WWW and the generally-recognized format for URLs. The format that follows is based on the APA manual, with modifications proposed by Russ Dewey (http://www.gasou.edu/psychweb/tip-sheet/apacrib.htm).

It's important to remember that, unlike the MLA, the APA does not include temporary or transient sources (e.g., letters, phone calls, etc.) in its References page, preferring to handle them in in-text citations exclusively. This rule holds for electronic sources as well: email, MOOs/MUDs, listserv postings, etc., are not included in the References page, merely cited in text, for example, "But Wilson has rescinded his earlier support for these policies" (Charles Wilson, personal email to the author, 20 November 1996). Note that many listservs and Usenet groups and MOOs actually archive their correspondences, so that there is a permanent site (usually a Gopher or ftp server) where those documents reside. In that case, you would want to find the archive and cite it as an unchanging source. Strictly speaking, according to the APA manual, a file from an ftp site should be referenced as follows:

> Deutsch, P. (1991). "archie—An electronic directory service for the internet" [On-line]. Available FTP: ftp.sura.net Directory: pub/archie/docs File: whatis.archie.

However, the increasing familiarity of Net users with the convention of a URL make the prose description of how to find a file ("Available FTP: ftp.sura.net Directory: pub/archie/docs File: whatis.archie") unnecessary. A simple specifying of the URL should be enough. So, with such a modification of the APA format; citations from the standard Internet sources would appear as follows:

Ftp Site

> Deutsch, P. (1991) "archie—An electronic directory service for the internet." [On-line]. Available: ftp://ftp.sura.net/pub/archie/docs/whatis.archie.

Gophersite

Massachusetts Higher Education Coordinating Council. (1994) [On-line].
  Using coordination and collaboration to address change. Available:
  gopher://gopher.mass.edu:170/00gopher_root%3A%5B_hecc%5D_plan

World Wide Web Page

U.S. Fish and Wildlife Service. (1996) Program overview. [On-line]. Available: http://www.fws.gov/~r9endspp/programs.html

Appendix 3

GLOSSARY OF USEFUL TERMS

Archie An Internet service that maintains and catalogs information stored on anonymous ftp sites worldwide.

ASCII American Standard Code for Information Interchange; the computer codes for the 128 text-only (numbers, punctuation marks, upper- and lower-case letters) characters.

AltaVista A popular **search engine** for the World Wide Web; others are Yahoo and Infoseek.

attachment A **binary** file attached to a mail message for sending over the Internet.

bandwidth A metaphorical term for how much information can flow through a specified point at any given time.

BBS Bulletin Board System; a computer system that provides its users downloadable files and discussion areas.

binary A type of computer file that contains non-text data; may not be sent over the Internet without conversion.

Binhex A common type of routine on Macintosh computers for converting **binary** files to text for Internet transmission.

BITNET An early supernetwork of academic computers; now mostly encompassed by the Internet.

Boolean operators A set of logical words used in boolean algebra to combine sets of objects or data into larger or smaller sets. Specifically, AND, OR, and NOT.

browser A **client** program that enables one to access and navigate the World Wide Web, either by clicking the mouse or pressing certain keys. Examples are **Netscape,** Mosaic, and Lynx.

client The program or computer that interacts with a **server.**

command line   A type of system that requires you to type commands to the computer to operate it; also called a Command Line User Interface (CLUI); contrasted with Graphical User Interface such as the Macintosh or Windows where you click on an icon or menu choice.

compress   To make a file smaller before transferring over the Internet to save time and **bandwidth.**

dial-up   A type of computer connection to a network that uses a modem and telephone lines.

Directory   1. A type of search engine that lists hierarchically arranged websites to allow browsing rather than searching. 2. In Unix and VAX computer systems, a location on the computer where a number of related documents are stored together.

DNS   (Domain Name Server) The computer that knows the addresses of all the other computers on the Internet.

download   To get or retrieve a file from another computer.

emoticons   The combination of punctuation marks that, when viewed sideways, resembles a facial expression that would otherwise be lost in text-based communication. For example, :-) is a smile used to indicate benign intent or "I'm just joking."

FAQs   Frequently Asked Questions; lists of questions that seem to appear over and over again on BBSs, Usenet groups, etc.; compiled and regularly reposted to cut down on the number of **newby** questions.

flame war   A nasty, often vulgar, exchange of insults over the Internet.

flaming   Being particularly vicious or personally insulting.

ftp   File transfer protocol; a method used for transferring data over the Internet.

GIF   A standard format of compressing and converting graphic information (i.e., pictures) to ASCII. Files with names ending in ".gif" are GIF files. The most common format for transferring graphical information over the Internet.

gopherspace   All the computers in the world that are networked and accessible by Gopher.

header   Gobbledygook at the top of email or Usenet messages.

hit   An item found as the result of a search query. The complete set of items found is called the "hitlist."

homepage   The starting point for a World Wide Web site; the first page you see at a site.

host   The computer you connect to when you access the Internet.

HTML   Hypertext Markup Language; the set of codes (or "tags") inserted into a document to make it usable over the World Wide Web.

http   Hypertext Transport Protocol; the language World Wide Web computers use to communicate with each other.

hypertext Non-linear writing in which the users follow associative links rather than reading from beginning to end.

IP Internet Protocol; the set of guidelines used by all computers for transferring material over the Internet. Also used to refer to a type of connection which places a desktop computer directly onto the Internet and allows for graphical Internet applications such as Netscape and *Eudora;* contrasted with text-only "shell" account.

IP Number The unique numeric address assigned to every computer on the Internet; consists of four sets of digits separated by periods, called a "dotted quad."

IRC Inter Relay Chat; an Internet tool that allows real-time written conversations to occur among many users.

ISP Internet Service Provider; where you get access to the Internet.

Kermit A method of transferring files from one computer to another; named after a small green animal which can transfer information faster than Kermit can.

keyword A descriptive term you enter into a **search engine** to try to find information; similar to Yellow Pages headings, for example.

listserv A software program that automatically handles the work associated with mailing lists, such as distributing mail to all subscribers. Occasionally used to refer to a mailing list itself. Other similar programs are Listproc and Majordomo.

log in (verb) To identify yourself, using your user ID and password, to a **host** computer.

lurk To read the messages on a listserv or Usenet group without contributing.

MOO MUD, Object Oriented. A type of **MUD** (defined later) which allows for meaningful objects to be placed in the room.

MPEG Motion Pictures Export Group; a file format for compressing video.

MUD Multiple User Domain. A place ("room") on the Internet where live, on-line chats occur.

Nettiquette The unwritten but sometimes fanatically adhered-to set of conventions and rules of behavior on the Internet, such as "don't type in all capital letters."

Netscape The most popular **browser** for the World Wide Web; others are *Mosaic, Microsoft Internet Explorer,* and *Cyberdog.*

newby Any new (and therefore unsavvy) member of an Internet group.

page A single document, regardless of length, on a World Wide Web site.

post To send a message or response to a Usenet newsgroup or **listserv.**

PPP Point to Point Protocol; a method of directly connecting one's desktop computer to the Internet. Similar to **SLIP.**

Query   A carefully constructed phrase made up of **Keywords** connected with boolean and other logical operators to describe the set of information you're searching for.

quoting   To reproduce a portion of a message (email, newsgroup, **listserv**) within the text of your reply so that readers know to what you are referring.

search engine   A program which will search the Internet for information you request. Popular ones are **Veronica** (for Gopher) and AltaVista (for the World Wide Web).

server   A machine on a network that provides information and services to the **client** computers that are connected to it.

signature   Identifying lines added onto email and Usenet messages you send, usually containing your name and email address. Some may be elaborate.

SLIP   Serial Line Internet Protocol; similar to **PPP** but older, a method of directly connecting one's desktop computer to the Internet.

spam   To send the same obnoxious (or commercial) message to millions of people at once. Highly frowned upon.

TCP/IP   The combination of Transmission Control Protocol and Internet Protocol; the language that allows computers on the Internet to communicate with each other.

terminal emulator   Software that allows one computer to act like another one, usually a VAX **VT-100,** the standard Internet terminal.

thread   A related group of Usenet or discussion list messages, consisting of an original post and all the responses to it.

Unix   A very powerful but difficult to use operating system for certain computers. The majority of mainframe computers on the Internet use Unix, unfortunately.

userid   User ID; the name assigned to you when you receive your Internet account, used for **logging in.**

uucode   Another standard, similar to **Binhex,** for converting **binary** files to **ASCII** files for transmission over the Internet.

URL   Uniform Resource Locator; the combination of mode and domain name used by the World Wide Web to connect to sites and browse or retrieve information.

Veronica   The **search engine** for Gopher; allows users to search **gopherspace** by typing in a number of **keywords.**

VT-100   A very early model of terminal for connecting to Digital Computers; obsolete, but this interface has become the standard.

Zmodem   Like Xmodem, Ymodem, and **Kermit,** a method for transferring data from one computer to another; Zmodem is the most advanced, the quickest, and the most reliable.

INDEX

Credits

This is a continuation of the copyright page.

Figures 3.1 through 3.4, 5.1, and 9.1 are reproduced with the permission of Digital Equipment Corporation. AltaVista, the AltaVista logo, and the Digital logo are trademarks of Digital Equipment Corporation.

Figure 5.2 is reprinted by permission. Infoseek, Infoseek Guide, Infoseek Your News, and the Infoseek logo are trademarks of the Infoseek Corporation, which may be registered in certain jurisdictions. Copyright © 1995, 1996 Infoseek Corporation. All rights reserved.

In Figures 5.3 and 5.4, text and artwork are copyright © 1996 by Yahoo!, Inc. All rights reserved. Yahoo! and the Yahoo! logo are trademarks of Yahoo!, Inc.

Figure 5.5 is reproduced with the permission of Carnegie Mellon University, copyright © 1994, 1995, 1996. All rights reserved.

Figures 5.6 and 7.1 through 7.5 are reproduced with permission. Webcrawler © 1996 America Online, Inc. All rights reserved.

Figures 5.7 through 5.11 copyright © 1996, Open Text Corporation. Used with permission.

Figures 6.1, 6.2, and 6.3 are reproduced with permission of Dartmouth College.

Figure 6.4 copyright © Bunyip Information Systems, Inc., 1993, 1994, 1995.

Figures 6.5 through 6.8 are reprinted with permission of the Regents of the University of Minnesota.

Permission to print Figures 7.6 and 7.7 was granted by CompuServe Incorporated.

Fig. 8.1, the Internet Public Library (http://www.ipl.org/), is reprinted with the permission of the University of Michigan.

Figure 8.3 is reprinted with permission of Cognito, Inc.

Figures 4.1, 9.2, and 9.3 are reproduced with permission of the Deja News Research Service, Inc. All rights reserved.